Praise for
Freddie: The Rescue Dog Who Rescued Me

"When I met Freddie in Vancouver, it was love at first sight. There was something about his expressive golden-brown eyes that seemed so wise and insightful as he sized me up. To my relief, I passed the Freddie test, and we were instant friends—something I didn't realize he reserved for a lucky few until I read Grant Hayter-Menzies's resonant tribute to this most special dog. In learning about Freddie, we also learn about Hayter-Menzies's life, and how both overcame overwhelming obstacles—in part because of each other. Their profound bond is something anyone who has ever loved a dog will understand. Freddie was a small dog, but he was larger than life, and this true tale is an inspiring, heartwarming read."

MARIA GOODAVAGE
New York Times bestselling author of *Doctor Dogs*,
Top Dog, *Secret Service Dogs*, and *Soldier Dogs*

"This heartfelt and charming book tells the story of how Freddie, a special little dog adopted from the BCSPCA, overcame his difficult start in life and learned to be a dog and best friend. Grant Hayter-Menzies illustrates the beauty of the human–animal bond in his reflections on how Freddie and the other animals in his life have influenced his writing, including biographies of several famous pets. Rags, Muggins, and Flush all make an appearance in this personal, insightful, and surprising account of just how much dogs mean to us. You will feel like Freddie is with you long after you finish this touching book."

ZAZIE TODD
PhD, author of *Wag: The Science
of Making Your Dog Happy*

"*Freddie: The Rescue Dog Who Rescued Me* details the life of a much-loved and engaging four-legged member of Grant Hayter-Menzies's family. This is not just a story about a dog—it is very much the author's personal journey. Freddie was a creature who needed special care but, in receiving it, gave boundlessly back to his carers and changed the author's own perception of being."

CHRIS CZAJKOWSKI
bestselling author of *Lonesome: Diary of a
Wilderness Dog, Harry: A Wilderness Dog Saga,* and
eleven more books about living in the wild

"I'm a sucker for a good dog story and this one is about as good as it gets. For, as the author notes in his riveting tale, 'Freddie would become something of a poster dog for the transformative power of love.'"

LESLEY CHOYCE
author of *Around England with a Dog*

"The story of Grant and Freddie's journey touches the heart of the human–animal bond. It is about love, adventure and making it through the difficulties in life with a friend at your side. It is a rich tapestry filled with snippets of history but mostly about the deep connection between the souls of a man and his dog as together they travel through life. A beautiful story."

CAROL HINE
founder of Senior Animals In
Need Today Society (SAINTS)

"Grant Hayter-Menzies has written a moving gem for anyone who loves a rescue. *Freddie* is a heartfelt story of trust, love, patience, and perseverance learned from one fearful Pomeranian. It's a tribute to life's surprises: sometimes you don't get the dog you imagined, but you get the dog you needed."

E.B. BARTELS
author of *Good Grief: On Loving
Pets, Here and Hereafter*

Freddie

THE RESCUE DOG
WHO RESCUED ME

Grant Hayter-Menzies

Heritage House Publishing Company Ltd.
heritagehouse.ca

Cataloguing information available from Library and Archives Canada

978-1-77203-461-5 (paperback)
978-1-77203-462-2 (e-book)

Edited by Lenore Hietkamp
Proofread by Nandini Thaker
Cover design by Setareh Ashrafologhalai
Interior design by Jacqui Thomas
Cover image: Oil portrait of Freddie,
by artist Vicky Bowes, 2014. Author's collection.

The interior of this book was produced on 100% post-consumer recycled-
paper, processed chlorine free, and printed with vegetable-based inks.

Heritage House gratefully acknowledges that the land on which we
live and work is within the traditional territories of the Lkwungen
(Esquimalt and Songhees), Malahat, Pacheedaht, Scia'new, T'Sou-ke,
and W̱SÁNEĆ (Pauquachin, Tsartlip, Tsawout, Tseycum) Peoples.

We acknowledge the financial support of the Government of Canada
through the Canada Book Fund (CBF) and the Canada Council for the
Arts, and the Province of British Columbia through the British Columbia
Arts Council and the Book Publishing Tax Credit.

27 26 25 24 23 1 2 3 4 5

Printed in Canada

This dog only, waited on,
Knowing that when light is gone,
Love remains for shining.

ELIZABETH BARRETT BROWNING
"To Flush, My Dog," from *Poems*

One should count each day as a separate life.

FORTUNE COOKIE MESSAGE
FOR FREDDIE
Moon Festival, 2011

To Freddie and Rudi,
with love for both—
and to Les
for believing Freddie would still be there.

With gratitude
to all the animal companions
who made my life richer,
and to Niko,
our newly adopted dog,
placed in our arms a year to the day
since we held Freddie for the last time.
Sweetheart, you have his eyes, and our hearts.

In memory of Muriel Jones, whose Holly was the only dog
Freddie didn't fear, and whose Welsh cakes he loved.

PART TWO

Foreword

As we shape shift, moving in and out of our suits of skins, feathers, scales, and fur, we maintain the consciousness that is "nurtured" and "natured" by our brief visits to the phenomenal world. Hopefully, while doing so, we effect positive change in those we touch. It is what Freddie as a dog exemplified and what Grant as his dad reveals in this homage that is not just to Freddie, who died in his Papa's arms, but to all loving relationships.

Freddie's life began as a Dickensian horror story and was transformed by the affection of three dads, Grant, Les, and Rudi. All four received what they gave—a greater sense of self-worth and the principle of enduring love, which blesses us in both the time we know as life and the place of memory, fixed in the words and photos of this tribute. This story is of the life of a rescue dog who became a rescuer as he charmed his way into the hearts of distressed and grieving humans, a narrative every reader will recognize as they revisit life as we know it, a world of laughter and tears.

Grant Hayter-Menzies is a biographer of the women and animals sometimes ignored in the grand scheme of great letters. His mission is to make sure these all-important stories are told, the lesson being that all life matters. In this time of discord, where animal heads are trophies and culture wars dominate the air space, he reminds us of the guiding principle of many North American First Peoples, *All my relations.*

One animal's head we will never forget is that of Freddie, carved into these pages, star of his own special book. Lest Freddie become a mere symbol, his father as author colors his pages with anecdotes from his own life and work, echoing the title of a beautiful film, *My Life as a Dog.* Who hasn't lived the life of Freddie as he experiences the vicissitudes of being and the transcendent moment when he approaches the golden door where dog is god?

This book is more than a memoir, more than an ode to love. It is a book of being that tells even more than it promises as it resonates in our hearts and minds. Grant's prologue, describing Freddie atop Glacier Point, resonates with all the possibilities of Freddie as he looks into the camera, the peaks of Yosemite behind him. Hard not to think of the Arctic peaks in the highly spiritual oeuvre of the great Canadian painter Lawren Harris, who heard the voice of God in snow.

Linda Rogers
SEPTEMBER 15, 2022

Prologue

Looking back on it, I can almost hear music: the shimmering sunrise in Ferde Grofé's *Grand Canyon Suite*, a perennial favorite of my father's, or the seismic tonal landscape, as violent and beautiful as the one we were in, of Igor Stravinsky's *Rite of Spring*.

Our car rose higher and higher above Yosemite Valley. The experience would surely have been a supreme moment in anybody's life, let alone that of the little dog sitting on my lap, his eyes shining, ears and nose pricked upward, toward the approaching blue roof of the sky. He had never seen such a place; and, it should be pointed out, such a place had never yet seen him.

A bit over a year earlier, Freddie, a Pomeranian cross of some fifteen pounds (making him, technically, a spitz), had been rescued from a world of troubles. He had spent his first year or two of life with an animal hoarder in the British Columbia interior, lacking sufficient food, veterinary care, and anything approaching socialization or, we had to assume, love.

We had adopted Freddie from the Victoria branch of the BCSPCA. He and his eight siblings had been shipped there via the Drive for Lives program, the aim of which was to find homes for every animal, even if that meant taking them well outside their place of origin. (Drive for Lives moves over 4,000 animals each year between BCSPCA shelters, to improve their chances of finding a new home.) In Freddie's case and that of his siblings, it was probably for the best that they be taken as far from the community of their rescue as was possible to go.

During his lifetime, Freddie would become something of a poster dog for the transformative power of love, all the more poignant and all the more inspiring for a pup who started out in what could not be described as loving circumstances. But then, not just that day but throughout his life, Freddie brought a palpable aura of luck along with him. It was worn, as Elizabeth Barrett Browning said of her spaniel, Flush, "like sunshine on his back."[1]

Yosemite Valley on that warm September day in 2011 was like walking into one of those too-perfect tourist calendar shots: sky an impossible blue, trees a vivid green, air pure and clear, growing purer the higher we rose. A winding road carved into granite, sometimes so vertiginous as to feel we were going straight up in the air, uncoiled snakelike before us. Our rental car, driven by my husband, Les, climbed through inky shadows of pine and spruce branches and splashes of bright sunlight to an almost treeless landscape.

From Freddie's predominantly black fur the beams picked out the silver, ginger, and even blue that gave his coat what his groomer called a "reverse brindle" pattern (an inheritance, as we discovered when we tested his DNA, from a Sheltie–miniature poodle great-grandparent).

He sat, dark triangles of ears erect, watching each new vista as it opened before his passenger seat purview.

Parking in the lot at Glacier Point, 3,000 feet above Yosemite Valley, we got out and stood a moment in the bracing breeze. The sweet scent of pine, the gritty, astringent aroma of lots of granite, and the almost too-pure oxygen at this altitude combined to form an ether, like inhaling some herbal wine, a retsina you could breathe. For me, this was a homecoming. I had been born and brought up not far from Yosemite, in the Sierra Nevada foothills, in the former goldrush town of Mariposa, which had caught my UK-born grandfather's fancy in the 1930s, the hills reminding him of certain parts of Scotland.

My father and uncle were the second set of twins known to have been born in Yosemite Park, which had at the time possessed the only up-to-date medical clinic for miles around capable of dealing with a thirty-two-year-old first-time mother of twins. It was here, one starry evening in late summer 1929, that my grandparents had met dancing on the valley floor to the strains of an outdoor orchestra, Chinese lanterns bobbing bits of color above their heads. No wonder he proposed two weeks later. She was a superb dancer.

Glacier Point was a favorite destination for my family, starting with the newlywed couple. They loved the old hotel (burned to the ground in the late 1960s) that perched on the edge of the cliff, its verandah giving views for miles of mountain ridges and sky, its lobby filled with comfortable wicker settees, upholstered in leather, and Persian carpets covering wide-plank floors. Here my paternal grandmother, Gertrude, had posed against the backdrop of Half Dome, garbed in an eighteenth-century–style silk shepherdess skirt, with a wide flowered hat and beribboned shepherd's crook, for a Roaring Twenties fancy dress ball.

Here—because there is a photograph to prove it—some time in the late 1920s, she'd also charmed a large brown bear. Calm, cool, and collected in her light summer dress and balanced neatly on the uneven granite surface in her French heels, she fed it a treat while male tourists, their necks hung round with binoculars, stood back, visibly afraid. They didn't know how benignly wild things would approach her—from deer in the forest to feral cats in town—without any more fear than she felt toward them. But I knew, and I could almost see her up there with us now, smiling at Freddie as another in a long line of beloved, characterful little dogs stretching back to her earliest known family history.

For Freddie, there was nothing familiar about this dramatic terrain. He was electrified, as if we had landed on a planet rich with heretofore unknown canine stimuli. To him, the wind was full of smells—wildlife and foliage he'd never known in Canada. Squirrels and other small critters scrambled over the rocks and up the rough bark of trees, unperturbed by crowds of tourists whose cars sat all around us in the lot.

Freddie's brown eyes were bright with interest as he pulled us, his halter and leash straining, up the slope to a high point where the hotel, and my grandmother, had once stood. The granite under our feet, undulant like billowing fabric yet sharp-edged like knives, glittered in full sun. Les got out the camera and I placed Freddie securely atop a boulder, so that he stood a bit above our heads against the cloudless sky.

At Les's urging, and with a tight grip on his leash and halter, I moved Freddie to face various directions, catching different angles of light. He patiently put up with this, looking out at each view with the wind blowing in his silky hair.

"OK, that's good," said Les, putting the camera away. I told Freddie, "We're done, sweetheart!"

That's when we heard the applause, interspersed with cheers.

We realized we were surrounded by tourists, representing at least a half dozen different nationalities, some pointing cameras at Freddie still sitting pretty on his rock, others just gazing up at him with smiles. We smiled up at him, too, emotion tightening our throats. Because a little over a year earlier, this little dog had been trapped in a cul-de-sac of pain. And here he was, literally on top of the world, healthy, well fed, and loved, the very sight of him the highlight of the day for these strangers who had never seen him before, might never see him again, but, I could believe, might not forget him. It would not be for the last time, and indeed, the smiles keep coming, though he is now as much a lovely ghost as my wildlife-charming grandmother.

Part of Freddie's enduring influence derives from the fact that on that day, I had an epiphany about myself as a writer as well as a human being. For several years, I had published biographies of extraordinary women— women like my grandmother, mentioned above, and like my mother, women of strength, determination, and compassion, whose gifts, while many, were insufficiently celebrated in a world where it was considered the mark of a lady to graciously allow herself to be interrupted— by men, by a child, by anything, even in the Swinging Sixties. My subjects were stage and screen stars whose groundbreaking careers spanned theatre, film, radio, and television; a defamed Asian female ruler whose governance was better than misogynistic western historians would have us believe; nineteenth-century women skilled in diplomatic finesse but nevertheless ignored; creative women who defended culture at great risk to their livelihood and sometimes their lives. I was telling their stories, but I was also writing about them to celebrate, by extension, the charismatic women in my own life who had made me the man I am.

When Freddie came into our lives in September 2010, my scope of interest in the unexamined life expanded to include the wholly mysterious, wholly engrossing lives of the animals with whom we share our nights and days, our wars, our beds, our love. I watched Freddie navigate normal life. He had to adjust to a level of security and care that must have been as unnerving as the grievous situation he'd been rescued from, because it was all completely unknown to him. He had to adjust to the love we gave him.

I had spent my boyhood and adult life around dogs— dogs who ate, drank, played, slept, ran, and so on, without the fears that beset Freddie at almost every turn. But now I saw that unless we taught Freddie how to be a dog, he would always live in fear, and that was heartbreaking. I was also filled with a justifiable but unhelpful fury toward the people he'd been rescued from, a reaction with consequences for my relationship with Freddie that he, and he alone, figured out how to remedy.

Freddie's inspiring ability to transcend his unhappy origins sent me into the pages of books, into official and personal records of lives stored in archives public and private—lives of animals as seen through the eyes of the human beings around them. That shift also guided me to see not only those lives from an animal's perspective but also how our tied destinies benefit them as well as exploit and harm them. And it took Freddie's last year, 2020–21, of gallantly pressing on through two cancer diagnoses and courses of chemotherapy and worsening heart disease, to see in the little dog who was present in my own life—not in the pages of books or newsprint— what canine courage really is all about. But most of all, it was his presence in the room as I wrote that helped me shift gears, to ponder deeply on the animal–human bond. "The kind of intimacy that a dog offers," writes Helen Humphreys, "is perhaps ideal for a writer, because intimacy with other humans often takes the writer away from their work, while intimacy with dogs brings a writer closer to their work."[2]

This book is not about me. It's about Freddie's extraordinary life, about how a dog caught in the vortex of exploitation and abuse was sprung out of prison and made a conscious effort to leave fear behind and welcome his new life with love. It's about how he taught me and so many other people who knew him what being free and giving love really are.

Yet, in truth, his life is about mine, because Freddie gave me reason to continue when, without him, I cannot say I would be writing these words, eight years later. In two of the most difficult years of my life, when an unrelenting pile-on of events gave me no reason to get out of bed in the morning and no incentive not to simply end it all, Freddie was the anchor that kept me here, the reason why neither flight nor suicide were options. I had to live for him, to fulfill my promise on the day of his adoption to always protect him and give him the life he deserved. Through living for Freddie, I discovered all the other reasons why it was important to continue living for myself. Through divorce, household moves, nervous breakdowns, and a score of other human-centered, human-created problems, I learned how much one little dog could do to, in the words of Emily Brontë, "centre both the worlds of Heaven and of Hell."

Like the dogs I'd only read about, those who refused to leave their humans despite disaster and instead stuck closer to them, Freddie was with me every step of the way. In contemplating the writing of this book, I intended to read through all eleven years of journals and correspondence relative to Freddie, as well as revisit the diary I'd kept from July 2020 to October 2021, following his cancer journey from beginning to end. My job as biographer, after all, is to document every step I take in the writing of a life. I did this, re-reading many of the books I had studied over the years (listed in the back of this book), trying to understand Freddie, trying to understand myself. My main goal, which I hope I have achieved, is to bring to life the dog who helped me when I was down and gave my career and my life purpose and meaning.

Without Freddie, I would likely have continued to write about human lives, but I probably would have come to a point where I wondered what else there might be, to what useful ends my communicative abilities might be turned. But now I know what that usefulness is. All the books I've written about the lives of animals do more than raise awareness, which was my original intention. They also raise funds—I donate a portion of my royalties from sales of these books to animal welfare charities here in Canada and around the world. Through them, Freddie keeps on giving.

This book is an appeal to all who may be thinking about adopting a special needs animal. When you go to your local shelter, please consider not just the rambunctious and outgoing dogs but the shy, the frightened, the shut down. When you save a life, you change more than the life saved. You change your own. That's what this book, and Freddie's life, is all about, and it's also what all our lives can be about—human lives and animal lives. Give a special dog a chance. You won't regret it.

PART ONE

CHAPTER ONE

Dogs of Memory

I CONSIDER MYSELF FORTUNATE TO know the name of a horse who lived on an ancestral farm in the colony of Virginia three and a half centuries ago. According to the will of Henry Culpepper, one of my maternal ancestors, the grey gelding was called Jack. That's all we know. However, when you read through dozens of old family wills and inventories and their lists of nameless, featureless equines and other animals important to the prosperity of a farm who pulled carriages to weddings and funerals, ploughed field after field after field, and ferried their owners to new lives, the mention of that one-syllable name and the color of Jack's coat means a lot.

I have a photograph my maternal grandmother, Nina, gave me of a horse on her father's farm in Texas, taken during the First World War. "His name was Will," my grandmother told me. Her father would put her on Will, she said, even when a prim great-grandmother visiting from Louisiana rushed down off the porch to say, "Charlie, no! She's riding *astride*!" (My grandmother was only three years old at the time.) "He was a sweet old boy," my grandmother reminisced. She was to become a proper elderly lady herself, but her great-grandmother's criticism that day was, for her, unreasonable and indeed unthinkable.

I wish I knew the names of all the animals that peer out at me from the black and white netherworld of other old family photos. My family clearly loved them. Why did nobody write them down? The namelessness of the horses, donkeys, dogs, cats, and birds felt to me like the time a reverend, having trouble pinning down his notes at a windblown lectern at the cenotaph one blustery Remembrance Day, mangled the names of some of the lost soldiers he read out to us. Because their names were all that remained of these soldiers, it seemed to me to be the highest of responsibilities to read them correctly, firmly, truthfully—and the height of clumsiness to mess them up, or even something worse, like giving them a second death.

But when I guess at the number of dogs, especially, in my family history, I realize it would have been a miracle had all their monikers been preserved. Long before Freddie, there were canines stretching back over the breadth of time. They were remembered by name, when known, but mostly just by details of their lives, by their individual personalities, recalled at Christmas dinners or when I was seated with an elder by the fire. What made this immortality of a short-lived species so special was that the person recollecting these dogs lived long after they had died and had only heard about them from a prior generation, also deceased, yet when I was told about them, it was as if they had been reincarnated in my mind, my heart.

The love handed down from one generation to another allowed these dogs some modicum of immortality, which helped compensate for the loss of their names in the present. There was the collie, Joe, who slept beside the stove in the kitchen of my maternal great-grandfather's cotton farm in east Texas. He followed the children—my grandmother Nina and her sisters—everywhere. One day, Joe dove into a pond on the farm to save my grandmother's toddler sister. He pulled the child out, to be revered as a hero evermore. My grand-mother treasured his memory all her life. She also forever pondered the mystery at the end of his. One morning, the old dog to whom she'd said goodnight the evening before was gone. As an adult, she wrote a story about how she imagined Joe's experience of his last night with them.

> In Joe's own mind, he knew that it was not only good-night, but goodbye forever.
> A little later, when the house was dark and quiet, Joe cautiously arose from his bed. Walking very care-fully until he was out of earshot, he slipped away like a shadow into the night. "Oh, my legs are so weak," he thought, "but if I am to get away before they know the worst, it must be done now."
> Some distance away, he turned to give one more long, last look at the house, and then slowly started on into the gloom of the forest.[1]

Knowing that Joe was aging and in pain, Nina reasoned, he had spared his human family the anguish of his immi-nent death by disappearing. She was spared Joe's death, but not the wondering about what had really become of him, and for the rest of her long life, she saw him in the eyes of every dog she came to love.

Dogs of Memory

My paternal grandmother, Gertrude, had a penchant for small dogs, apparently a family trait going back centuries. One of her German ancestors from the fourteenth century was Tamburga von Schlüchtern gennant Katzenbiss, a surname Tamburga discarded for her husband's less tongue-twisting one of von Hutten. After her death, which occurred some time before 1355, Tamburga was memorialized in the shadowy family chapel with a carved effigy of her lying on a slab, clothing draped just so, rigid in anticipation of meeting her maker. Yet there is a bright major note in this darkly minor dirge. At her feet is a comically lovable dog who could have been conceived by Walt Disney, displaying all the goofy geniality of Pluto. A not uncommon feature of memorial carvings, an effigy dog was so placed as a symbol of religious fidelity, and a sculptor would often go to great lengths to give it character. Some of my ancestors are shown with little dogs pulling at a deceased lady's skirts; one lady was depicted holding one. Tamburga's dog is portrayed in the way we, who love them, see dogs—charmingly unselfconscious, prone to the prankish play they know will amuse us and earn themselves a treat as payment for the performance. And so it would be for future generations. In paintings and photographs of my grandmother's German forebears, a dog always appears, with all the regularity, in Victorian times, of a piano and potted palm in the corner.

I have a photo of Gertrude taken in 1914 in Los Angeles, spiky shadows from palm branches splayed across her floral print dress as she holds a very young puppy, one of a litter of three born to her beloved Boston terrier. In a later photo, taken in about 1974, a few years before her death, she holds another young dog, a

Chinese pug called Cindy. The joy expressed in the early photo varies as little from the later one as the way she positions her arm to cradle the pups six decades apart. The love had not changed.

As mentioned, Gertrude had an affinity for animals, both wild and tame—bears or deer, or the animals she found on her father's three hundred acres in the Imperial Valley, where around 1915 she was photographed hugging a steer. I have a memory of her in her eighties, arthritic, in pain, but making a daily journey down a flight of steep stone steps behind the house to the neighbor's field, where a lonely jenny (female donkey), similarly elderly and infirm, waited for her and the bowl of vegetable scraps my grandmother always had for her. Seeing these two elders, limping painfully toward one another, their gray heads touching as Gertrude offered the bowl of treats, was unforgettable, as was the fact that on the day my grandmother died, the old jenny stood in the middle of her field and brayed her loss for hours.

As with Nina, Gertrude also had a sad memory of a dog that remained with her whole life. Some time in the 1900s, she recalled, she had tied a red ribbon around the dog's neck and ran out to the garden with her to play. The dog raced across the lawn and into the unpaved Los Angeles street, where she was struck and killed under the wheels of a passing streetcar.

There were similar tears when my father told me of the stray, Peanuts, that he had adopted as his beloved companion in the early 1950s, when he was recovering from a divorce. One morning, Dad told me, Peanuts crawled into his office and died at his feet, poisoned by a dog-hating neighbor. "If I had only known how little time he had left," my father told me, in his eighties and only a few weeks from death himself, "I would have loved him more."

The very atmosphere of my birth and childhood was infused with animals. My first recorded word ("bird-ee," according to my mother's notes in my baby book), at six months, was inspired by the canary that sang in its cage in our living room. I haunted the cage, watching its every movement with delight, a fascination that continues to this day.

Our home housed all kinds of other animals besides the canary. A pony, Dickens, who liked to come inside our house, did so once when my grandmother Nina, a very proper Southern lady, happened to be visiting us. My mother saw Dickens coming and gestured to me to ward him off, but it was too late. Dickens clopped up to my grandmother, stretching out his muzzle toward her, and she, who'd been talking to my mother, reached out and caressed it without missing a beat. She said to him warmly, as to a guest late to tea, "Hello, my dear, how are you?" I never knew why my mother was worried. Nina adored horses. Though she was a devout Christian for whom the Hindu concept of reincarnation was foreign, she told me once that she hoped there was something to the idea. She wanted to be reborn as a wild horse, running forever over green fields.

Along with the canary, other birds, and Dickens, we had at any given time guinea pigs, hamsters, fish, cats, and rabbits. When any of the small animals died, my parents helped us with their funerals, Dad making little wooden caskets lined with cushions that my mother sewed from satin scraps. We stood at the graveside in our back garden, weeping freely, reading from whatever page the Bible opened to, and the death was treated like that of a family member—because it was.

In my memory, though, it's the dogs who stand out most.

As a baby, I spent hours with our black and tan dachshund, Wiener, born in June 1964, the same month I was born. In the miles of home movie film my father shot, Wiener appears frequently, deftly dodging demonstrations of my sandbox authority as I ward him off with my spade from digging more holes than I could. There he is at Christmas, running around the tree alongside me and my younger sibling in gift-opening frenzy, patiently allowing my mother's Siamese cat to bat at his wagging tail.

And all the other dogs: Sissy, our snow-white Samoyed who knew how to shake hands and was a cunning prankster; King, the quiet old collie cross who once had found and brought home my toddler cousin, who had wandered into the woods, when even the sheriff's deputies couldn't locate the child; and Rama and Veda, the saluki hounds given to me by a relative, with their feline grace, cheetah-like speed, and sweet natures. There were neighborhood mutts like Dude, who looked like a dustmop and was not much tidier, our joyful companion during childhood forays into the hills and creeks around our town, always up for adventure.

The night Nina died, in January 2001, my sister had a dream. She saw our grandmother sitting in our childhood garden, surrounded by every animal companion we had ever loved—Dickens the pony; dogs King, Sissy, Rama, Duchess; cats Boots, Squeaks, Waif; our hamsters and guinea pigs and birds. She was the only one of us three grandchildren to have such a dream, but it was one we understood, a heaven we could believe in, because we had lived it, with all of them.

Dogs of Memory

I moved to Canada in 2006 as a permanent resident, having married my Canadian husband here on Vancouver Island in the summer of 2005. Our seaside wedding, with its pennanted tents and kilts and harpist playing tunes from my Scots grandfather's songbook, would have been complete had our dog Jessie been able to join us, as we had planned and hoped. The idea was to have her carry our rings, tied to the lace and satin ring pillow from my parents' wedding almost forty-five years earlier, in a basket as part of the wedding party.

But Jessie, who had been a ball of energy her entire life, beginning with her rescue as a stray in Sidney, north of Victoria, some seventeen years earlier, was beginning to fade. A true island mutt, she was something of a cross between blue heeler, German shorthaired pointer, and possibly Dalmatian, with God knew how many other varieties blended in. In fact, Jessie was about the same age, in dog years, as a friend of ours, a lady in her nineties, who told everyone at our reception how delighted she was to have finally attended her first gay wedding. If only Jessie could have been there, too.

Her energy gradually ebbed. Though we were able to manage her arthritis with pain medication, her joints grew stiffer; it was harder for her to walk any distance. After attempting to slowly climb the stairs to our bedroom, Jessie began to find more comfort in sleeping on a mat we made for her in the living room, in front of the fireplace. She had grown more deaf, and her eyesight was no longer acute, not to the point where she went completely blind but in the way a very old human being has to feel her way through a room. Bright light seemed to make not for clarity but confusion. And then came the subtle but increasingly obvious changes in Jessie's acuity.

Years later, my godfather, Bill Luce, went through a five-year battle with Alzheimer's disease. In most ways that count, it was not so different with Jessie in 2008, except that, for Bill, we had to see him through his struggle to the end. With Jessie, we had the blessing of knowing that a call to her vet would stop her suffering before it overwhelmed her and us. The other struggle? Knowing when.

One night, I discovered her under the dining table. She had somehow wandered in among the table legs and chair legs and could not find her way out again. She didn't bark or cry out. She simply stood there in the shadows, waiting to be found. Even more troubling were the episodes in which she would wander into the corner of a room and just stand there. These incidents were as much a part of Jessie's decline as her inability to control her bowels and bladder. I remember coming downstairs one morning to the sight her of her standing amid mess, trembling. I soothed her only through touch because she could not see or hear, and by then it seemed even her sense of smell was lost. She seemed to exist in the half-light of waiting—waiting for us, not to find her when she'd gotten lost but to find a way to end her suffering.

Finally, one day, Les called Jessie's veterinarian, Dr. Nigel Bass, and an appointment was made.

We took her to the beach, gave her the steak and treats that we'd had to hold off for so long because of her tricky digestion. We then drove to Dr. Bass's office. Les laid her down on an examination table that we'd covered with one of her blankets. We stroked her head, and as she became drowsy from the sedative, we were asked if it was time, and Les nodded. This elderly dog, who lay utterly prone, her eyes gazing out at the clouded indefiniteness that had been her world for some months, now lifted her head, and her eyes, suddenly as clear and liquid as if her sight was restored, focused intently on Les, and stayed fixed on him until the second injection flowed into her veins. When Dr. Bass took Jessie away, he carried her in his arms like a baby.

At home, we opened the door to that emptiness anybody who has lost a dog of many years will recognize. But we both also had a strange sense of Jessie's presence. "She's still here," Les said. "She came back with us." Having learned about Chinese customs for commemorating the dead, I placed Jessie's water bowl, her kibble, her leash, and her collar on the mat before the fireplace, the way a Chinese family might leave a bowl of rice and incense before portraits of their ancestors at Qingming, the Clear and Bright Festival in spring—food for body and for soul. As with all such ceremonies, at least it comforted us.

During that week, we lived in a house that, had you asked us, we'd have told you we did not occupy just for our two selves. The volume of a living presence seems to displace space, and for those seven or eight days, it felt as if Jessie was with us, a sense that that space was still being occupied by her. Don't ask me how—I tend to pivot between wanting to believe in the continued presence of our loved ones in spirit form and knowing, on the solid floor of reason, that when we die, it's over.

Or is it? Because on the morning when we awoke and both said, almost in unison, "Do you feel that? She's gone," a call came from Dr. Bass's office. Jessie's ashes were ready for us to pick up.

Some days later, we scattered them, along with her leftover kibble and water from her bowl, into the calm waters of a little beach she loved, watching as the tide carried them away.

CHAPTER TWO

Homecoming

EVEN MARRIAGES THAT SEEM to begin like fairy tales can have bumps in the road—can end, even, the way no fairy tale should, though many of the most famous ones do. My parents had met under romantic circumstances, but they had had a volatile relationship all the years I knew them. It seemed they couldn't live either with or without one another, trapped in that vortex that keeps people together despite the misery they create for one another, because alongside the misery is that stubborn superglue, love. I never understood that process until I experienced it, and contributed to it, myself.

Mom once told me she stayed with Dad because of us; she was of a generation that believed divorce was worse for children than staying together. Dad once told me he remained in the marriage because he adored his wife as much as he had the day he first saw her and told a friend, "I am going to marry that girl."

When Mom's mental health issues began to surface, in the form of acts of self-harm, of mania followed by depression, he knew he could never leave her. To this

day, I have a memory of Dad carrying my mother, uncon-
scious from an overdose of the prescription pills her
doctor had liberally prescribed for her, out of our house
and down to the car, roaring off in the night to get her to
hospital. It was the first of several hospitalizations and a
glimpse of what was to shorten her life.

During those dark nights of my childhood, our
animal companions were more important than ever. I
sometimes sat with Wiener or King or my guinea pigs
and told them about everything I feared. When they
gazed at me, their palpable innocence both moved and
comforted me, reminding me that when everything else
in my world seemed to be unreliable and unstable, the
reality they lived in seemed the opposite, forever above
the fraught human fray.

My picture of marriage, unfortunately, was not an
ideal or even a friendly one. A veteran of several relationships that had not panned out as hoped, I had grown
accustomed to a freewheeling bachelorhood in Portland,
the thin but glamorous solace of premieres and first
nights as an arts journalist reviewing opera, symphony,
dance, art gallery openings, and the parties that went
with them. But when I fell in love with a Canadian, and
it grew serious to the point of proposal, and equal marriage became the law in Canada, I said yes. How not to
love the man who swooped into my life and gave me a
chance to build a healthy partnership, having learned
what not to do from my parents' example and my own
mistakes? Together, we had a chance, in our forties, to
make a beautiful life together in our home with picket
fence and antique furniture and dog Jessie as our child.
But after she left us, a period unfolded of first being
drawn together by her death and then parted by what

her death triggered in us, and the first cracks in the perfect portrait of wedded happiness began to appear.

Among many who have divorced, you will always find some who will tell you that they didn't see it coming. I didn't. In fact, the shock of being told my marriage was no longer viable was truly a sandbag to the head, a stunning that could last for years.

With us, however, all that had yet to come. We shared some strong shared interests, personal and financial, and we still cared for each other. And it takes courage to break a vow made to one another before happy friends and family. So our rickety ship, now missing the steadying presence of our mascot Jessie, continued to sail on.

We traveled the world, we worked on projects, entertained friends and family. Les supported me through all my writing projects, from research to book launches. But something was missing. It wasn't just Jessie, but it was a lot about Jessie. And this is probably why Les was perusing the adoptions page of the British Columba SPCA website one evening in September 2010.

We had talked occasionally of adopting another dog, even while Jessie was alive, though we ultimately decided that introducing a younger animal into Jessie's household would have been unfair to her, when she was happiest with peace, quiet, and the two of us. We had looked now and then at the lists of adoptable dogs, sometimes disappointed that the one we'd fancied was adopted within what seemed like minutes after being posted. The photo Les asked me to come look at that evening at the computer was, to my mind, the same as all the others.

Founded in 1896, the BCSPCA started out for the same reason many other animal welfare organizations in the Victorian age did: to alleviate the suffering of working equines, who in those days pulled carriages and carts and milk floats and ploughs, and operated grinding mills and other machinery before mechanization. The organization seized animals the law had determined to have been abused, providing them with veterinary care and lobbying for more laws to protect them, as well as recommending penalties for convicted abusers.

I had known heroic people associated with the SPCA in the United States. One woman of my acquaintance, affiliated with the SPCA, had been alerted by a concerned citizen to the plight of a neglected dog left tied perpetually to a post in the yard of a ramshackle residence outside a town. With insufficient water in the heat of summer and insufficient shelter from the cold in winter, and paradoxically grossly overweight from being thrown whatever scraps of junk food the owner did not consume, the dog was in a bad way. Yet the local police couldn't be convinced by the citizen or the SPCA that this animal was being abused and must be taken from the man. The concerned citizen understood that, as animals are considered property, to free the dog from its circumstances would be considered theft under the law. But to leave it there to live and die in misery was impossible. So a decision was made between the woman and the citizen, and one morning, when the owner came out to toss the dog some scraps, it was nowhere to be found. The dog, given a full examination and put on a diet, its matted coat shaved and rotten teeth removed, lived several more years in another state, in a caring home. When the time came, the dog passed away in loving arms.

While I do not condone vigilante solutions to animal neglect, I'm not sure I wouldn't have done the same myself. An illegal action can also be a moral one, and this act saved a suffering dog's life. As was said of Dorothy Brooke (1883–1955), who founded the working equine charity Brooke Action for Working Horses and Donkeys (the subject of my 2018 biography, *The Lost War Horses of Cairo*), compassion gave her the authority to interfere— to step over the cordon sanitaire and take matters into her own hands. As we were to learn, such compassion in action had played a significant role in saving Freddie.

That night at the computer, Les said, "Look at this pup. He's like a wee fox. His name is Frederick." I stood behind him to see, leaning in for a closer look. I saw a small, fluffy dark dog who did, in fact, look foxlike: his sharp triangles of ears were down in fear, and fear also veiled the bright brown eyes glowing on either side of a sharp triangle of a muzzle.

The text attached to the photos went like this:

Frederick's Details

TYPE: Dog
BREED: Pomeranian Cross
SEX: Male
COLOUR: Black/Brown
AGE: Young Adult

Below this information was the caveat reminding us that to prevent disappointment, we must realize that the website was live, updates were frequent, and the dog we wanted to see this evening might not be there in the morning or might even be in process of being adopted as we arrived on site.

"What do you think?" Les asked. "We can go see him tomorrow morning." We had errands to run in Langford, but we could make it to the Victoria branch on Napier Lane around noon, he figured.

I confess I wasn't sure. Jessie was still in my heart. I had known people who adopted another dog or cat soon after an earlier companion animal died, and while it seemed to go well in most cases, some found their decision had been made too soon and had complicated the path of getting to know their new family member. Not even two years had passed since Jessie's death. Shouldn't we wait a little longer? But I was intrigued by the foxlike dog being held up to the camera, his sad eyes and demeanor pulling at me: the gravitational force of compassion, and of pathos.

I said, "Sure, let's see him. But I'm sure he'll be gone by the time we get there."

"It's worth a try," Les replied.

BY THE TIME WE reached Napier Lane, we'd spent a couple of hours in Langford dealing with home improvement chores: selecting curtain rods to fit two sizes of windows on the ground floor of our townhouse; looking at area rugs, faucets, and sinks, and tile for kitchen and bathroom.

For a while now, Les and I had been talking about renovating our place, then selling up and moving not just from Sidney but from British Columbia entirely, entranced by the low cost of properties in eastern Canada. We focused on areas where we believed Les could secure another government job and where I might be able to work at part-time day jobs so as to have more time to write.

By the date of our visit to the BCSPCA shelter, I'd published three books and was in the process of researching and writing three more. I was earning good reviews, if not royalties sufficient to allow me to leave full-time work behind. We thought that could be easily remedied by taking our west-coast equity to the more reasonably priced east coast. In fact, my thoughts were much more focused on this scenario than on adopting a dog. I had worked for a few non-profits in Victoria since arriving in Canada in 2006. Grateful as I was for the work, none of them called on the skills I'd been well paid to use when I lived in the United States, and this caused financial problems for us that I had not foreseen, adding to the strain of our marital situation.

I had groused, but as many immigrants must, I accepted this reality of working at jobs for which my skills were under-utilized, especially after I learned more about the circumstances of new Canadians who were more highly educated than I. A handsome elderly taxi driver who had ferried me to some meeting, the minutes of which I was not looking forward to taking, had a Ralph Vaughan Williams symphony playing on the stereo. We soon engaged in conversation about music. He was delighted to hear I was a trained pianist, while I was delighted to hear he'd been a professor of music in Afghanistan. His parting words, after we'd sat in the cab conversing, would stay with me for some time: "As long as you love music, you will always be happy." Thanks to him, I resolved to be more patient with my lot in life. If a former doctor of music, forced to flee his homeland, could be happy, as long as he had music, ferrying people around town who did not comprehend what a mind and heart they had at the wheel, then I had nothing to complain of.

But in truth, it wasn't so much the freedom to write itself that was making me eager for change. It was that

I was increasingly dissatisfied with the kind of writing I had come to specialize in: the lives of women. Not that I was no longer interested in writing about and celebrating women's lives—far from it, and I would continue to do so in several more books, published in Canada, the United States, and the United Kingdom. Perhaps it was in part because the women I was attracted to writing about were people who sought to change the world not just for their own gender, but to find solutions for the plagues of poverty, exploitation, and cruelty that affected all life, both human and animal.

My suffragette great-grandmother, Nettie Lodewig Launspach, of San Francisco and Los Angeles, had helped win the vote for Californian women. She was also concerned about deeper issues at the root of some of society's social justice problems: the double whammy experienced by women hauled to jail on morality charges who were then at the mercy of male guards and policemen in that setting, some of whom took advantage of them, making a mockery of the law. Nettie fought to force San Francisco to allow a woman to put herself forward for police commissioner, and she also put pressure on the city to allow women to serve as police, the better to deal with women arrested in what was very much a man's world with men's rules.

Like many social justice activists, she also loved animals and deplored the abuse of them. When I was researching for my biography of dog-loving Lillian Carter, the mother of President Jimmy Carter, I had dinner one evening with the Carters and told them about Nettie. "You should be writing about her!" said Rosalynn. She had a good point, although one of the reasons I wanted to write about Lillian Carter was because I had a Nettie

in my family tree. However, I wanted to deal with the
spectrum of social justice issues beyond the realm of specific movements—how, for instance, a suffragette could
march and be arrested for equal rights while at the same
time arguing for more compassionate treatment of animals. How it was possible to care about all beings whose
dignity and freedoms were threatened, human or animal, without identifying with a particular cause or camp
or fashionable movement. How every unexamined life
deserved to be taken seriously.

In essence, I was searching for a new form of biography, one that would take me outside my own comfort
zone, that would depend on methods outside the box,
and that would, I hoped, fulfill me in ways the current
format was increasingly failing to do. Perhaps, too, this
restlessness had as much to do with our obsession with
moving away from Vancouver Island as it did with the
fact that I, and probably Les, thought that such a move
might have the knock-on effect of saving our marriage.

Our west-shore chores done, we pulled up to the
one-storey stucco building at 3150 Napier Lane, with its
blue and yellow BCSPCA sign. We walked into the lobby
and asked to visit the adoptable dogs. Les and I were
directed to the kennels through a door behind the shelter's reception area. The entire facility has since received
a makeover, but what I recall from that first visit in 2010
is a long hallway, the walls painted a neutral color associated with utilitarian purposes, with similarly neutral
fluorescent lighting above.

In the kennels area, we looked for the chain link
gate, of which there were several lining each side,
interspersed with painted cinderblock walls, that was
supposed to bear the name card of Frederick, the dog we

were interested in. To find it, of course, we had to look at each gate, which meant also meeting the eyes looking back at ours—eyes of poodles, terriers, Alsatians, labs, mutts; eyes hopeful, frightened, sad, wary. It would have taken a heart of stone to ignore what those eyes seemed to say: Are you the one? Have you come to get me?

We looked at every gate and saw nothing labeled "Frederick." "I had a feeling he'd have been adopted by now," I murmured, recalling the ginger Pomeranian we'd passed as we entered the building, being taken away by an adopter. (Later, we found out this had been one of Freddie's siblings.) We assumed this was a hint of how popular the breed was and, again, how unlikely it was that Frederick was still here. Sadly, all the other dogs on offer were too large for our strata's size limit. The visit felt pointless, as I'd feared it might be.

I turned to leave. Les noticed a kennel attendant and stopped. He asked her if a dog called Frederick was still here, explaining that we couldn't find his name card. "Of course he is!" she smiled.

She led us back down the corridor between the kennels to one we had already passed. Its gate bore a white card that was larger than the others to accommodate the name Ichabod. When the attendant pulled it to one side, underneath was another card, on which was printed "Frederick." He was still here.

At the small opening between the public and private sides of the kennel stood a tousled white Maltese, too small to carry the weight of such a moniker as Ichabod, that unhappy biblical name. He looked up at us, not as if to ask if we were the ones and had we come to get him, but rather with a vaguely annoyed air, as if in judgement of our readiness to give up, to lose hope so easily when we were surrounded on all sides by the hope that endures despite everything.

He ran to the opening in the back of the kennel where another dog peered out, black where Ichabod was white. The attendant knelt at the gate and called brightly, "Frederick!" And through the door emerged a small, thin, dark-haired dog, with fluffy curled tail and bright brown eyes. "Here he is!" said the attendant.

The dog was clearly expecting to see her, not us, and he drew back. He only came forward again, slowly, as the attendant coaxed him to the gate. Evidently, he had formed a bond with her. For each animal brought in, the BCSPCA performs an assessment to determine a number of facts about a rescued animal, quite apart from the medical examination. Is the dog socialized? Was there trauma in the dog's previous setting? Was the dog likely to be adoptable sooner or later, depending on all these factors? This attendant, whom we later came to know better, had helped bring Frederick out of his shell. We were a complete unknown, however. We later came to recognize this cautious behavior as Frederick's propensity to give men a wide berth, leading us to conclude that he had been abused by a man at some point in his first year or two of life.

"Just pick him up," said the attendant. "He'll be fine."

I held Frederick in my arms. He shook in every bone and sinew and was unwilling to look at me or at Les, in a replay of his state when he'd been photographed for the branch adoption page.

"He's a loving guy," said the attendant, looking at me and then Les intently, as if she feared we were having second thoughts. She need not have worried. As the small body trembled against my chest, I already knew.

Homecoming

"We want him," I managed to say.

"Let's take him outside," suggested the attendant, "and see how he is with you both."

We emerged from the shelter into the golden warmth of the afternoon, Frederick now wearing a collar and leash. I put him down on the grass. The first thing we noticed was how unfamiliar to him all the things familiar to us appeared to be. He stood on the lawn as if he had rarely or never felt the soft green stuff under his paws before. (He would later have a similar reaction to snow.)

Frederick glanced with curiosity and some wariness at the cars flying past on Burnside Road East below. He started when a breeze blew his fur, and when a seagull swooped overhead, he gazed at it in open-mouthed wonder. What sort of awful circumstances had this quiet, fearful little dog been rescued from?

In the lobby, I sat with Frederick on my lap as Les filled out the adoption papers. He was not trembling as much as before, but his heart pounded against mine. I looked down at his scrawny body, fur trimmed presumably because of matting, and those liquid eyes, golden brown like the smoky onyx brooch my mother wore when I was a boy. Frederick sat poised, somewhere between fear and anticipation, as I too balanced myself unsteadily, between the utter pathos I felt for this traduced innocent creature and hatred for the human beings who were responsible for him being here, for his being this way.

What was his story? What had rendered a healthy young dog, a year or two old, so terrified of all the essential mechanisms of ordinary life, everything I had ever known and unquestioningly accepted? Frederick's trembling made me speechless with rage at the monsters who had done this to him. As Les returned with our copies of the adoption forms, putting his pen away and readying to go, Frederick pulled away from me, trying to reach Les.

"What will you call him?" asked the receptionist.

"Let's stick with Frederick—he seems to know it best," Les said, as the dog gazed up at him. "But how about just Freddie?" he added, caressing his head. On the drive home, as I held Freddie, all he had eyes for was Les.

Alexandra Horowitz wrote, "Trying to understand a dog's perspective is like being an anthropologist in a foreign land." Little did I know that for both Freddie and me, finding a method of communication between our two perspectives would be the biggest challenge of our first months together.[1]

CHAPTER THREE

"A Country Stranger than the Moon"

T'S AUTUMN 1972. I am eight years old, and I am about to sit on an elephant.

The setting is the Sierra Nevada foothills of central California, where an elephant has no logical reason to be, where ground squirrels, cattle, and blue jays are the approved resident fauna. But the elephant is a star attraction, brought here as part of a roadside sideshow featuring numerous wild animals—tigers, apes, a bear. The sky is bright blue above rolling golden hills stippled with the sticky dark green of scrub oaks. I am so gleeful I seem to have floated rather than walked up the path from the parking lot.

She astounds me at first sight. Standing about five feet high at the shoulders, she is a small-eared Asian youngster, a buff gray color, dusty from working in the grassless red dirt of the park. Like me, she is a child, maybe between eight and ten years old. Elephants are one of the few animal species that share our lifespan, even our stages of development, as well as elements of our vaunted intelligence.

As I look at a picture taken of her that day (and having shown the photo to elephant experts, who know more about them than I ever will), I can see that while she is neither underfed nor in physically poor condition, the elephant is very tired. Since long before I'd arrived near the end of that day with my mother, grandmother, and siblings, drawn by the roadside sign, she had been ferrying several children at a time on her back, to which was strapped a trekking seat set atop a bright Persian carpet. Hers had already been a day full of obeying her keeper, retracing a circumscribed route while being mindful of children placed astraddle her spine. Though her eyes droop, they are remarkably beautiful, set in perfect circular creases, their tender amber irises fringed in long lashes.

A loud man is in charge of this quiet elephant. He asks my mother if I want to ride her. I am all for it, of course, but my mother says I may do so only if she can stay near me, walking alongside, as she does when I ride ponies. The keeper tells her abruptly that, no, she may not walk with the elephant but must ride with me, or I won't ride. My mother doesn't like that idea—or his tone. An experienced and sensitive horsewoman, she is bothered by the idea of putting more weight on the elephant's back than seems normal for her to bear. As these negotiations go on, the elephant stands there almost motionless, patiently staring ahead.

My mother at last agrees, under pressure from me, and a wooden step is produced. That's when the keeper gets out his stick. He suddenly raps the elephant on the face and calls a command. I feel my mother flinch. The elephant kneels, and my mother helps me on. I sit just behind the elephant's head, in the mahout position.

Then Mom easily hoists her slender self up and sits just behind me, holding me steady. We are all ready to go when two older boys clamor to be allowed to join us. The keeper jovially encourages them to "jump on." My mother wants to dismount, but it's too late. Carrying three children and one adult, the elephant is rapped again by the man.

As the elephant stands, my mother whispers something under her breath; I know she is angry. But I am unable to concentrate on anything except the fact that I am sitting on an elephant, and we are moving. She and we are led by the keeper in the same circle she has been treading all day, yet to me our brief trek is magic: I become Rudyard Kipling's Mowgli in my Madras shirt and buckled back-to-school shoes. I feel a strange oneness with the elephant, who now is a large, broad head in front of me and a large, broad body under me, as she takes careful steps at the keeper's bidding, walking in a rocking motion that for me is mesmeric, comforting. I feel her neck and shoulder muscles shift and roll under me, feel the buoyancy of her breath. The forest my imagination had conjured from my books at home now surrounds us, just me and the elephant, as we traverse a jungle together, quiet but for birds and beetles and the trees weaving over our heads.

Our ride actually lasts just a few minutes. When the elephant brings us back to the wooden steps, the keeper gets out his stick again and raps her on her leg and on her face. For the instant it takes for my grandmother Nina to snap a photograph, the elephant lifts her trunk in a winsome curl, her left leg in a sort of salute. Then she kneels, and we get down.

As soon as she touches the ground, my mother asks the man why he had to strike the elephant. He says something I can't hear, but I gather he tells her that his is an inscrutable profession, the mysteries of which no layman could understand, and how he handled the elephant is his business, not hers. My mother is upset to see anyone hurt an animal, and she loathes men who speak patronizingly to women. So we depart the park under a cloud of her regret that she had ever brought us there in the first place.

At the car door, I look back at the elephant once more, just in time to see her being rapped again to kneel for more children screaming for the chance to sit on her.

THERE IS A REASON why I share this memory. This event was the first time I had ever seen an animal mistreated, under the guise of it being "professionally handled," but it was not my mother's first time. She had seen horses abused and had called out the abusers. Her anger from those memories were linked to what she felt the day we rode the elephant. She felt she had set a bad example by letting me get on. Years later, she told me that it was clear the animal was not well looked after, and she thought that making the elephant perform tricks as well as carry kids around all day, without rest, was ridiculous and cruel. "I thought of you before I thought of her," she said.

But she had wanted me to experience an amazing animal that I might never be so close to again, not realizing the situation till it was too late to back out. I remember what had happened just before we left. My mother had stopped an employee of the roadside circus to complain about what she had seen, had been blown off with laughter and scorn, leading to strong words, and to my mother crying as she drove us away. For years,

I couldn't look at the photo of us on top of the elephant, nor could my mother. And in truth I had not thought of it for a long time, until we brought Freddie home from the shelter, and all the old sadness and anger welled up in me again.

Our Sidney townhouse seemed a storybook forever home for an adopted dog. It had a picket fence around a secluded garden, with shrubbery and small trees for shade, brick pavers, a fountain. The rooms of the house were spacious and airy, the floor covered in soft carpets and antique furniture, comfortable and inviting, with a staircase winding to the second floor that Freddie, in time, was to enjoy dashing up and down.

Yet for almost an hour, that first day, Freddie sat in a corner of the kitchen, his face down, eyes averted, shaking in fear. When we tried to comfort him, he lowered his head further, as if expecting to be hit rather than caressed. Les said, "He just needs time," and I realized that was the case. But I looked at this small creature, shaking and withdrawn, afraid of his situation and of us, and I began to spiral into the old place of seething hatred for people who abuse animals, a place I had not experienced for years and which now I could not escape.

When I told my parents about Freddie and that he seemed to have been not just neglected but abused, my dad said, reasonable as ever, "Well, son, he's with you guys now, and that's all that matters." My mother thought the same, but she shared my anger. "I'd love to have five minutes with whoever did this to that poor pup," said the woman who, frail and ill, had just two years to live.

The signs of Freddie having spent his first few years in some abnormal setting were rife. When we offered him a toy, he leaned back, afraid. Les and I both were shocked: we had never known a dog who did not instinctively know what to do with a toy, who did not respond to an invitation to play. When we rolled a ball across the floor, he watched it with apprehension. We showed him where his food and water were. He would lap at his water quickly, always looking at us, and grab kibble in his paw and run with it to the safety of the underside of a bench or table, where he would eat it while eyeing us warily. He also displayed severe separation anxiety, which was never really allayed by the passage of time. "If you were to construct a scenario guaranteed to foster the development of separation anxiety," wrote Dr. Nicholas Dodman, "it would involve the impersonal rearing of batches of dogs in an environment where social contacts were scarce and close bonding with humans is virtually impossible." Dr. Dodman also notes a tendency in these dogs to hoard their food until their owner comes home—an exact description of what happened when, to distract Freddie from the fact that we needed to step out to the grocery store, I gave him a special treat, usually a Dentastick, which was like handing a chocolate bar to a child. He didn't receive these treats daily, weekly, or even monthly, as a rule, but he knew they were in the cookie jar shaped like an English bulldog, and his eyes shone at the very sound of the crinkling package as we retrieved one for him. But on our return, invariably we found Freddie sitting on the bed, waiting for us to arrive, the stick upright in his paws and untouched. He'd greet us with joy, then fall upon the Dentastick, tossing it into the air and catching it in his teeth before settling to wolf it down.[1]

All of this seemed to indicate that Freddie had had to fight for his food and that the humans in his environment had not been kind. We also concluded that he had not been socialized at all. On walks in Sidney, Freddie would rear back at the sight of other dogs, once jumping into Les's arms and urinating down his shirt when a too-friendly collie ran up to us.

"He doesn't speak dog," I said to Les. "I don't think he knows he's a dog." Who could do this to an animal? I asked myself this question often.

Gradually, in the coming days, Freddie began to open up. We'd stopped just putting a toy in front of him. I thought if I showed him what a dog should actually do with it, he would understand not just the process of play but the fun of it. His cautious brown eyes watched me, at first somewhat alarmed, as I picked up a toy in my teeth and shook it madly, crawling away just as madly. (I thought of these "lessons" when, a few years later, I wrote about Rags, the former Paris stray and mascot dog of the United States First Division in World War I–era France; Rags, too, had been taught by his American soldier rescuer to run dispatches through shellfire and hellfire, carrying them in his mouth, as if they were a kind of toy. All formally trained dispatch dogs carried messages in metal cannisters attached to a collar around their neck, never between their teeth.)

I remember the moment when Freddie caught on. At first, he batted the toy with a paw; when he'd lobbed it far enough away to make it exciting to pursue, he chased after the toy, carrying it back. When we tried to take the toy playfully from him, he held on for dear life, and then started shaking the toy back and forth, though it must be said he never damaged his toys except super-ficially (which meant that, by the time he died, all the toys we gave him over the course of eleven years were still largely intact). He also quickly developed the skill of learning the names we had given to each of his toys. He could tell the difference between Green Monkey and Funky Monkey, pulling whichever one we asked him to find from the growing contents of his toy box.

I also remember when a ball became a thing of joy to Freddie. From watching it warily as we rolled the green sphere over the floor, he took immediate interest when it tipped over the edge of the stairs and bounced inexorably down to the floor below. Racing after the ball, Freddie carried it back up to Les, and from that moment on, ball was his favorite game. He loved it best when we took him out to a soccer field where he could chase it over a broad expanse of grass, that surface he had been afraid to step on the day we met him at the shelter. The sight of his energy, joy, and fearlessness was a relief.

Something else, though, was troubling me. Freddie was not bonding with me. We had acquired an old but informative book from the early 1930s, *Our Friend the Pomeranian*, that seemed to explain the breed's temperament: "A stranger . . . need not expect any demonstration of affection from the dog, but merely a good-natured tolerance."[2] But this situation was different. I wasn't quite a stranger, and even if that had been the case, Freddie was not showing me "a good-natured tolerance." In fact, I wasn't sure he even liked me.

His manifest attachment to Les was lovely to see—after all, for his first few days with us, Freddie had kept his distance from us both; it was a relief to see him respond to affection. But I didn't appear to be included. It felt to me as if the more I touched or held him, the less Freddie wanted signs of affection from me. This was even more baffling because my way of showing love was different from Les's. I was demonstrative, as I'd been with pets and people since childhood. Les was more self-contained, disciplined; he didn't push you away, but he wasn't into displays of affection. Yet Freddie adored him and kept his distance from me.

The problem reached the point where I decided professional help was needed. I called Janet Parker of Clever Canine, a canine training and behavior consultant in Victoria.[3] "I work with people who love their dogs," I read on her website, "but not their dogs' behaviour." In our case, as I explained to Janet, it wasn't that Freddie misbehaved—he was keen to learn new things and obey rules. For a dog from his background, he had learned to walk on a lead and do his business outside rather than inside with astonishing rapidity. It was not an issue with bad behavior. It was that he didn't seem to like me, and I wanted to know why.

Twelve years later, we talked about that day. "When I think about your initial relationship with Freddie, and how he seemed to have chosen Les instead of you," Janet said, "I think there are a couple of things at play. Freddie needed someone to survive . . . he just happened to choose Les. You very desperately wanted to connect with Freddie and you wanted him to connect with you. That can look like anger or frustration, and it creates a lot of pressure, the pressure to be 'better' for the dog, and pressure for the dog to 'hurry up and like me.' We all do it, but dogs don't like pressure. And may respond by shutting down and/or avoiding situations or people."

Janet's advice for how I could establish trust with Freddie was to hand-feed him his meals, every day, for as long as it took.

So we began.

I sat cross-legged on the tiled floor of our kitchen, holding Freddie's food bowl in one hand and feeding him chunks of its contents with the other. At first, he was baffled, as well he might be. But the canned delights we bought for him were too tempting to worry too much about how he received them, and soon we had settled into a routine, me in my post-work business casuals on the floor, Freddie sitting close by to get his supper, bite by bite.

The ease with which he was adjusting to new experiences—and this was certainly a new one for us both, though, as I would find out in years to come, it would also be a feature of our last weeks together—was heartening. But his indifference toward me did not change. Even so, I was prepared to do anything to overcome it and gain his trust. And while feeding him, it was wonderful to have him close to me, for even a short while. So I kept on.

I also tried to do some work on myself. I remained haunted by memories of the tired elephant of my childhood, to which were added many other unforgettable images, made worse by the internet's 24/7 availability of more of the same. I had joined various Facebook groups dealing with the welfare of animals wild and domestic. Because I found so much information pertinent to Freddie, I followed other groups formed for hoarding and puppy mill survivors and how to help them, as well as campaigns aiming to put mills out of business and their operators in jail. As with so many of these groups, while they provide a great deal of useful information and camaraderie, they also fill your head with terrible images of animal suffering.

I am one of those people for whom a photographic memory is more curse than gift. The sight of animals in pain and suffering (which would ultimately prompt Les and me to go vegetarian, another by-product of Freddie coming into our lives) stayed with me and stoked my anger at the abusers. In turn, this transferred to anger toward whoever had made Freddie's life hell prior to his rescue. It was a circle I couldn't seem to break.

One of my favorite saints is Francis of Assisi (d. 1226). I was brought up by nonconforming parents who adjured us to choose a religion if we wished, or desist if we preferred it that way, and as a result, my siblings and I remained at an interested but noncommittal distance. What I loved about St. Francis was his respect for animals, treating them with the same respect he accorded to human beings: by taking them seriously.

About a month after we'd adopted Freddie, I had a dream. Before I fell asleep, I had been cogitating over a horror story in the news, in which a dog had been beaten almost to death by a mentally disturbed individual. (It eventually had to be euthanized.) While still alive at the emergency veterinary hospital it had been taken to, though paralyzed, the dog had tried to wag its tail for its caregivers.

When I said the elephant was the first time I had seen an animal abused, it was not the last, and that night I recalled another incident from my childhood. When I was about thirteen, my brother, sister, and I found a dog. It had been tied to a tree and beaten viciously and left to die. We later heard the perpetrator was a prominent local man angry that the dog had come onto his land, but nothing more can be said because in small towns like ours, people of consequence operated to a set of rules different from those imposed on everyone else. All I remember is that the battered animal, who was shortly after euthanized by the sheriff's deputies, called to the scene by our mother, also tried to wag his tail.

These two dogs, victimized by human madness yet greeting their helpers with gratitude, were among the many memories that often kept me from sleeping. But that night, they faded to the background, and I slept.

I dreamed I stood at the bottom of a low hill, in a darkness like the twilight before dawn, sun creeping up behind but not yet spilling over the crest. I was watching dogs of all shapes and sizes, dogs whose fates had broken my heart but who were now well and whole, padding up a path to a figure standing at the crest of the hill. The figure wore a brown robe and looked suspiciously like the medieval St. Francis figure we had on display in a glass cabinet downstairs. The figure reached out and touched the head of each dog as it approached him and then moved on past him toward the dawn light.

That was all, but it was immense, because though I woke up in confusion, the sense of relief was overwhelming. I felt completely different, as if the anger and despair I'd been humping around like an overstuffed backpack had been lifted off my shoulders. I could see things as they were in the now, the way Freddie viewed the world, no matter his sad beginnings. I recall thinking, "I've done it! The anger is gone. I can let it go. Freddie will know and will come to me now."

But he didn't. Life went on much as it had before, with the exception of me hand-feeding him with a greater sense of purpose, expecting nothing from him, refusing to allow unreasonable, useless emotions to cloud the space between us.

In fact, I felt fine just letting Freddie be; and when Les departed for a three-day business trip to Calgary, I didn't hover. I went on with my life, working at my desk, walking and feeding Freddie, doing household chores, getting in an hour at the piano (another new experience Freddie came to enjoy, sitting under the instrument as I played). It was just a blessed wonder to feel free, and Freddie seemed no worse and likely better for me not trying to make him do or feel what he didn't want to feel or do.

The evening before Les's return, I was sitting on the floor upstairs, rearranging books. These were placed on shelves along one wall, floor to ceiling, extending the length of a long hallway. It was getting dark, but as usual, when shelving books, I ended up reading one of them, and I couldn't be bothered to stand up and turn the lights on.

I was reading a poem of Babette Deutsch, "To Helen Keller," written in 1931, and the first lines struck me as particularly pertinent to my situation with Freddie:

> You live in a country stranger than the moon
> Where nothing casts a shadow. In that place
> Night has no secrets, and the ripened noon
> Sheds only empty warmth upon the face.

In trying to communicate my love to my dog, through all his complexities and all my emotional whirlwinds, I sometimes felt like Annie Sullivan trying to reach the blind and deaf child Helen and find a way to help her understand the world she lived in, while trying herself to understand that world, to feel in the darkness for some way to understand each other, seeking shared light.

As I continued reading—

We have not known that country, save in dreams,
And they were terrible. How shall we then
Find ways to come to you across the streams
Of baffled sense?[4]

—I heard, through the words in my head, the clicking of Freddie's nails on the uncarpeted floor of the hallway. I glanced up and there he was, eyes keenly studying me from the shadows. "Hello, sweetheart," I said, touching his ears, which he increasingly liked us to stroke. Then I went back to the poem. Freddie came closer, sat on the floor next to me, and lay his head on my knee, looking up as if to say, "Dad, I'm sorry. I trust you now."

There was no way, between the Deutsch verse and the being who had chosen to show me unbidden affection, that I could control my emotions in Freddie's presence, and I wept. But these emotions weren't based in pathos or outraged feeling. I was thrilled to be living in the present moment—where all the best poetry comes from and where all animals are most comfortable—thrilled to be really with this little dog who had chosen to make me a friend. "To live with a dog," writes Dr. Marc Bekoff, "is to know firsthand that animals have feelings. . . . We also know that we're not the only sentient creatures with feelings, and with this knowledge comes the enormous responsibility and obligation to treat other beings with respect, appreciation, compassion, and love."[5] I accepted that responsibility, with a gratitude I had not really felt till now. And never again did Freddie shy away from me.

CHAPTER FOUR

Seeking Truth

A BY-PRODUCT OF RESOLVING MY anger over how Freddie was treated prior to rescue was to begin a search for what that pre-adoption life had been like.

Part of me wanted to know the details, believing they could explain mysterious facets of his personality—his ongoing phobias, the bad dreams that woke him up, as if he'd been running in fear—and tell us something about the nature of a puppy mill and an animal hoarder, and provide some closure. The reason I start any of my biographies is to find out what made a personality tick, what events shaped a life, how crisis could trigger courage.

Of course, part of me didn't want to know. But if there was a chance that what I found out could help us understand the little dog we had taken into our home and family, I was willing to pursue it.

I was especially moved to do this after reading Kim Kavin's 2012 book, *Little Boy Blue: A Puppy's Rescue from Death Row and His Owner's Journey for Truth*. Puzzled by certain characteristics of the puppy she had adopted through a rescue that brought dogs up from the southern

United States to the north, Kavin traced the life of her beloved Blue. Born to a stray in North Carolina, he was pulled from a high-kill shelter, where he was on a list to be euthanized in a gas chamber, then fostered by a hoarder before he was driven to Pennsylvania, where Kavin adopted him. Her book is still a classic, not just because it showed the terrible circumstances in which many good homeless dogs end up, often killed before they have even had a chance to live, but also for the determination of a dog mom whose love of her boy led her into dark places in search of his origins and the fate of so many dogs like him.

I decided to start my own dark journey on Freddie's behalf, and I began with a friend I'd made through the BCSPCA. I'd come to meet Denise Meade through emails about Freddie's first calendar contest entry in 2012. Each year, the BCSPCA holds a calendar competition in which you enter your pet and ask for votes, which are tied to donations to the charity. We'd entered a photo of Freddie posing against a bank of orange azaleas in Seattle, where we'd taken him to see the Space Needle (Les and I had proposed to each other in the restaurant atop that monument years earlier).

By then, Freddie had made many friends in the Greater Victoria area and farther afield—in the United States, the United Kingdom, and Europe—and enough votes were cast to include him in the lineup of winning rescues for the next year's calendar. Finding herself on the island on business, Denise had gone to the effort of bringing us a copy of the calendar prior to release. We'd struck up a friendship after that, and I remember the day I decided to ask her the question: What could she tell me about the situation Freddie had come from?

Denise was resigning from the BCSPCA for a position with another animal charity in Alberta, but before
she left, she looked through Freddie's file. What she told
me was sobering. The animals on the property had been
observed living in neglect; there were also suspicious
newspaper ads listing them for sale or for free. Finally,
an anonymous good Samaritan had reported the situation to animal control and the BCSPCA came in to rescue
the animals.

There were eighteen dogs in total on the property,
but just nine—five Pomeranians and four Maltese—were
removed, Freddie among them, thankfully. Though the
conditions were said to have fit the definition of an animal hoarder, the ads alluded to activity characteristic
of a puppy mill/backyard breeder. The dogs were unsocialized, not neutered or spayed, and undernourished.
Ichabod, the Maltese we'd met in Freddie's kennel, had
been friendly and unperturbed by our presence, but
we heard that one of his littermates needed foster care
for another two months. He showed a complete lack of
social skills and had a fear of children and noise, freezing when overwhelmed, all of which Freddie shared,
including the habit of chewing on stuffies for hours on
end when anxious.[1]

Only toward the end of his life did Freddie's habit of
freezing and hunkering down in distressing situations
come to a stop, after we had worked with him for over
a decade. That this behavior was not isolated to one
or two of the dogs from the rescue site was confirmed
when I heard from adopters of three dogs from that
August 26 seizure. They, too, in the words of one of the
adopters, had to teach their adopted dog how to live.
One of the adopters, Crystal Labrie, is a certified Fear

Free technician (an initiative conceived by American veterinarian Dr. Marty Becker that is used around the world) and was on staff at the Kamloops BCSPCA when Freddie and the other dogs from his household were brought in that August of 2010. She had taken one of the Maltese into her home, a male called Brody. A few years older than Freddie, Brody's reaction to his trauma was to exhibit aggression, which made him, unless he could be helped to overcome this tendency, unadoptable and thus a candidate for humane euthanasia. Labrie told me this aggression was too often a rescue dog's downfall, through no fault of its own. Freddie hadn't lived in Brody's world as long; his reaction to trauma was to retreat, not resist—to appear to disappear, as Freddie seemed to be trying to do the day we brought him home. Labrie worked with Brody and he began to blossom. But, like Freddie, Brody remained triggered the rest of his life by a range of what we might consider normal daily stimuli—noises, changes in his environment. "In hoarding and puppy mill settings," Labrie said, "these dogs never learn who they are—that they are dogs. They serve other purposes, and their own welfare is never considered."[2]

The very word "hoarder" conjures squalor. The last years of Anna Anderson, the Polish woman who impersonated Grand Duchess Anastasia of Russia, daughter of Tsar Nicholas II, were filled with press accounts of run-ins with the law in Charlottesville, Virginia, over the disaster zone in which she and husband, Dr. John Manahan, lived. The formerly elegant house became filled with the detritus of years of garbage, tarnished tsarist memorabilia, and reeking animal waste from the dozens of cats that were given free run of the premises, many of them in poor health. A similar state of affairs was made famous by the 1975 documentary *Grey Gardens*, by Albert and David Maysles. Former socialites Edith Bouvier Beale and her daughter, Edie Beale, lived in a crumbling Long Island, NY, mansion overtaken by cats, raccoons, mountains of empty pet food cans, and waste of every kind. But one could still see the fine aristocratic bones of the house, its remaining furnishings, and the two women, going on their eccentric way in finishing-school accents and delusion, clueless about the suffering of animals that their lifestyle encouraged.

When I was in my teens, I knew a relative of my mother's who, now that I am middle-aged and have seen other cases, would probably be diagnosed these days as a hoarder of animals. My relative was the daughter of a famous United States naval commander and his wife, a fashionable woman who came from a background that straddled the worlds of high-class decorating, early silent film, and relations knighted abroad, a life for which one had to be not only well bred but also talented. My relative's mother also deeply loved animals, once bringing her parasol handle down sharply on the head of a man in the streets of post–World War I Istanbul when she caught him beating his donkey. She lived surrounded by dogs and horses, as did her daughter, the relative I knew, who inherited her mother's love of them. In her heyday, she kept a prestigious stable of Arabian horses and bred salukis from a lineage stretching back to desert sheikhs. She wasn't limited to dogs and horses: A tame llama lived on her property, responding to her calls made to it in Arabic and French; it would eventually be allowed to live in one of the house's many rooms, and often came into the living room where we were.

My relative was complicated, fascinating, infuriating. She had dabbled in dance and acting, was well read, and understood animals better than almost anybody I have ever known. But somewhere along the line, she lost the plot. For all her faults, she was a magnificent spirit, a brave survivor. But it has to be said she typified a signal characteristic of hoarders. Everything she did was based on preserving, collecting, and hoarding, whether objects, of which she owned and protected a vast number, treasures from prior generations that even in want she would not sell, or animals, which she similarly protected, despite being unable to give them proper care. For her, each object and animal had a story, and keeping them around her kept alive the people and dreams she had loved and lost. She genuinely loved her animal companions. She just didn't know how to do anything else for them but love them.

I had to wonder: Had Freddie come out of such a situation?

I learned that women—typically older ones, often with unresolved trauma in their past or present lives—made up the majority of hoarders known to law enforcement and animal shelters. One of the unanswerable mysteries of Freddie's life prior to rescue manifested itself to us soon after we'd brought him home. He was afraid of other dogs and would hide behind one of us should a person he did not know approach us on the street or visit the house. But I lost count of the times when Freddie would be drawn to women with white hair, wherever they appeared, approaching us, across from us on the opposite sidewalk, or walking ahead. Even years later, after he had benefited from socialization to conquer many of his initial fears, if he saw a white-haired lady slowly making her way, he pulled at the leash to go to her. The one dog Freddie never feared was an aged rescue called Holly, whom he even tried to play with, to our amazement. But even she seemed to be of interest to him because she was always with her guardian, our elderly neighbor, a lady with grey hair and gentle demeanor; she was a known quantity, not to be feared.

What did these women represent for him? Was there, in his sad early years, such a woman who showed him kindness? Could it have been the woman from whom he and his siblings were seized?

We even consulted a medium. The reason for this went back many years in my history. In February 1989, I was living in the Sierra Nevada mountains in a house almost twenty miles from the nearest town. A snowstorm had begun a few days earlier, and by Valentine's Day, everything was covered three feet deep. I'd lost electricity and was relying on candles and oil lamps for light and the fireplace for warmth. Late that night, through the wind, I heard what sounded like the crying of a cat. I went to look for it but the snow was coming down so thickly my flashlight was not of much use. I was preparing to turn in when I heard the crying again, this time closer, and realized there was a cat, or what appeared to be one, sitting on a little porch that was accessed from the bedroom through a glass door. I shone my flashlight beam on the most wretched-looking animal I had ever seen.

The animal, who proved to be male, once I'd got him dry and could see more of him under the matted fur, was a small Siberian forest cat, his coat gray-and-black brindle. His eyes were nearly shut, crusted over with infection, his nose ran, and his ears were clearly inflamed. I got him into a cat carrier and placed him on a leather sofa in the living room, where he could have the warmth all night from the fire, determined to get him to the vet next morning come hell or high water, if he was still alive.

He did survive the night, during which he proved he had excellent manners. Needing to urinate, the cat had figured out how to open the latch on the carrier, peed in the button tufting of the sofa, then returned to the carrier.

The veterinarian couldn't believe what he was seeing. He told me that beside being emaciated and dehydrated (the small bit of food and the water I'd given him the night before had probably saved his life), the cat had ear mites that had nearly reached his brain, and his eyes would need to be surgically re-opened. He also needed a total shave, as all his fur was matted in unpleasant lumps all over his body. "What kind of eyes do you want him to have?" the vet asked, since he was able to play God, in this instance with a scalpel. I said, "How about Elizabeth Taylor?" and sure enough, once his wounds healed, the cat I called Liebchen had the sultriest gaze of any feline in the world.

As Freddie would do later, Liebchen seemed to know when I was upset or in pain. He came to me unbidden, but this was no surprise. This cat, who had come in out of a snowstorm 4,500 feet up in the mountains, had a refinement, a sensitivity and awareness, that you would not normally expect from a stray. In my childhood, I had tried to help a stray cat that had got into our yard and whom I was feeding regularly. I managed to bring him into the house, only to have my hand almost scratched off. He raced madly around the room until I opened a door and out he went like a shot. Liebchen was different, a sort of lost prince exiled from his kingdom through forces he could not describe for me, bringing all that he had left, his elegant manners, with him (precisely like some elderly Russian aristocrats I once knew, who had been forced into exile and poverty by revolution). How, though, did he come to be this way? How did such a tidy, refined cat get lost in the middle of the woods?

I was writing at the time for a weekly paper, and my editor happened to be in the neighborhood, so she came by for a visit. A woman of great compassion, wit, and bravery, Ariel was delighted to meet Liebchen, and he clearly felt the same, jumping up and making himself at home on her lap. "You know, I can sense things about animals," Ariel told me, stroking Liebchen, "almost as if they're speaking to me." She proceeded to tell me all the basic facts that Liebchen's medical stats had revealed to us but which she could not have known, such as an old injury to one of his ribs, along with several other details no one could have verified except Liebchen, who was content to focus his sultry green eyes on Ariel in thanks for her stroking.

Could we do something like this for Freddie?

We have all heard about desperate families consulting mediums to find lost children. An opportunity fell into our laps. Les and I attended a health fair in Victoria where we met and were "read" by a medium whom I'll call Sharon. I found it somewhat off-putting but also intriguing when, instead of telling me about me, Sharon said, "There's a small dog that you love very much. You'd rather be at home with him right now, wouldn't you?" I told her that was pretty astounding as, yes, there was a small dog and I had just been wondering if we'd been away from him too long. (Part of our effort to help

Freddie become more self-sufficient was to leave him home for an hour or two while we went out on errands, having turned a camera on to see how he did in our absence. When we watched the video later, we were happy to see him sleeping peacefully.)

Sharon asked if she could meet Freddie, and we arranged a date. When she arrived, we three sat in the living room, Freddie on the Persian carpet at our feet. Sharon told us things about Freddie that were fantastical because impossible to verify. But the animals she described as his friends on the rural property where, she said, he had lived were the very ones he showed no fear of now—cats and raccoons and horses, animals around which he always showed a peculiar comfort. She told us the property had a small stream, his only access to fresh water, and that someone would toss food to a group of dogs, and there was fighting over it. (Years later, when chemotherapy had thinned his coat, we saw old bite wound scars on Freddie's back.)

"He didn't usually get enough to eat," she said, "because he was afraid of the fighting." She said Freddie was communicating to her how happy and grateful he was for the home he had with us and wished the other dogs he had been with could know about it and have similar lives. "He's a magical little guy," Sharon said, looking at Freddie. "He's got healing properties. You have brought him good luck, but he brings you the same. Do you feel it?" (Weirdly, this, too, was something my mother had said to me on meeting Freddie months earlier. She also said, after I described Sharon's visit, "I could have told you that for free!")

I'd heard many of these types of statements and questions before. I was curious about psychic phenomena, a similar feeling I had in response to the question about whether there was life after death. While a heaven made sense to my heart, my head and gut told me that when we die, it's over. I still didn't know how to explain the feeling of Jessie's presence in the house that week before we received the call that her ashes were ready. That same uneasy curiosity moved me to reserve judgment on Sharon's pronouncements.

One thing that stayed with me was a vision she shared that gave Les and me chills. Sharon told us that she saw an image of Freddie "in a shelter of some sort, and he's hiding behind someone; he's afraid of all the other dogs. They are upset and don't know where they are." Following Freddie's seizure from the hoarder, almost the very hour he was brought in, the shelter photographed him and his siblings in the intake area, a photograph the shelter had shared with me. His ginger siblings mingle close to a volunteer who crouches down among them; they are clearly uncertain but apparently still able to function, as curious as they are fearful. Barely visible, cowering between the young man's knees, is the tiny black puffball that is Freddie, completely terrified of his surroundings. There was no way Sharon could have known this. In some sense, pursuing this line of "enquiry" left us more confused about what to think than before.

Freddie occasionally had what we thought were bad dreams. We've all seen a dog dream. As it lies sleeping, the tail starts to flop against the floor in a half wag, the paws go up and down, and the back legs kick. There are muffled woofs, even barks. It's easy to imagine that a dog displaying these behaviors is dreaming of play. Freddie's bad dreams were different. He would tremble and appear to be trying to escape something. He would whimper and cry. When we slowly woke him—it took a few minutes—he'd stare wildly, as we humans will do when we wake up from a nightmare, not sure if the terrible place of the dream is real or imagined.

I would often nap with Freddie on the weekends. I'd lie down on the bed, he'd jump up and nestle beside me, and I'd wake up an hour later with him still there. This was a great improvement from the days when he wanted nothing to do with me, and I treasured each opportunity to be close to him.

One afternoon, I fell asleep with my hand across Freddie's back. I dreamed of seeing two cages in a kind of basement or space with minimal light. They were set atop other cages. The cage closest to me contained a Pomeranian puppy with gray fur that looked only weeks old; the cage I could see through the interstices of the nearest one housed an older Pomeranian with a lot of ginger in its coat, as well as gray and black. The little one was looking at the older one and trying to get closer to the cage's edge but had trouble doing so because the openings in the cage were so large its paws kept falling through. The older Pomeranian looked stressed.

I awoke with my hand still on Freddie's back, and while I looked at him, he, too, woke up. He lifted himself and turned to look at me, and we lay like that for some time. A dog doesn't normally like to meet the eyes of another animal for an extended period. A fixed stare can signal aggression. Sometimes a dog will stare at its human to get something, usually the sandwich the human is trying to eat or the last bit of ice cream in the dish. Freddie was looking at me with that we called chocolate pudding eyes. His deep brown gaze was soft, welling, luminous. He was perfectly relaxed.

"Were you that puppy I saw?" I whispered, stroking his ear. "Did they take you away from your mum? I'm sorry they did that to you."

Writing about some of the prime causes a variety of fear-related syndromes in dogs of Freddie's background, Dr. Nicholas Dodman explains that "the trauma of early weaning alone can be enough to lay the groundwork for separation anxiety."[3] Such early weaning is an unfortunate hallmark of puppy mill environments. But I realized something, as we continued to look at one another in the quiet room. My obsession with tracking backwards to the source of his pain, making myself angry and upset in the process, had caused the problem between us which Freddie had since resolved by going against his fears to meet me where I was.

While researching *From Stray Dog to World War One Hero: The Paris Terrier Who Joined the First Division*, my 2015 biography of Rags, mascot of the US First Division, I'd visited the Maryland pet cemetery where Rags was buried in 1936. As I roamed among all the other gravestones, I found one marking the burial place of a collie, inscribed with a quote from a famous poem, "The Curate Says You Have No Soul," by St. John Lucas (1879–1934). In the poem, the narrator seems to be talking to the dog of his boyhood, who was barred from the family pew at church by the curate who, like many people in older times and many people even today, believed animals are soulless and therefore undeserving of Christian sacraments. The narrator decries this prejudice, believing—like Emily Dickinson, who hoped the first loved one she would meet on reaching heaven would be her Newfoundland dog, Carlo—that God could not be so cruel as to have devised a netherworld in which a loving dog, to whom heaven was unavailable, barked on dark hills in search of a master that he would never find. Lucas saw himself sitting in Charon's boat crossing the River Styx, looking forward to being a shade on the other side if only because there he would be reunited with his dog.

As Freddie looked at me, I remembered the words by Lucas carved on the gravestone: "I will not think those good brown eyes / Have spent their life of truth so soon."[4] I needed no evidence to tell me that willingly leaving the happy present for an uncertain and unhappy past was useless; it had almost cost me Freddie's trust. So I stroked his ear again, snuggled against him, and we both went back to a dreamless sleep, unconcerned with then, content with now.

CHAPTER FIVE

A Love Letter

NOT LONG AFTER FREDDIE came into our lives, at a time when I was discovering details of his pre-adoption past, I read a book that moved and inspired me greatly— Jana Kohl's *A Rare Breed of Love: The True Story of Baby and the Mission She Inspired to Help Dogs Everywhere.* Baby was a three-legged white poodle with shining dark eyes whom Kohl had adopted from Petfinder.com. She had been bred in a puppy mill, where the owner had had her vocal cords cut to silence her barking. But nothing could silence her eyes, which despite how humans had treated her up to Kohl's rescue, shone with the steady lambency of candleflame, communicating in ways her now silent voice could not.

A psychologist by profession, Kohl was drawn to animal welfare through an interest in social justice issues. Before adopting Baby, she had visited a puppy mill in Texas, an experience that was like walking into a horror film: cage after stacked cage, feces and urine from dogs above falling on those below, sores on feet and bodies. Manic barking and other behaviors were the pernicious by-product of being caged from birth, removed from mothers too soon, and offered no social- ization or even touch. All the dogs were merely birthing machines to feed the maw of unscrupulous pet stores that never asked questions about where the merchan- dise came from and made money hand over fist selling victims of the system to the unwitting or the unques- tioning. In Kohl's care, Baby blossomed, and she made something else bloom in Kohl—a crusade to put a stop to puppy mills by starting at the top of the pyramid of the nation's power structure, Washington, DC, and the politicians elected to serve the American people. With Baby at her side, and with the influence of a growing group of celebrity supporters behind her—politicians like Barack Obama, Ted Kennedy, Rick Santorum, and John Ensign (wisely crossing the aisle for help: ani- mals know no politics, and animal welfare should, in an ideal world, never come down firmly in any political camp), as well as animal lovers from other walks of celebrity life, like Judge Judy Sheindlin, Heather Mills, Montel Williams, and Martina Navratilova—Kohl lob- bied for the legal changes necessary to shut down these work camps for dogs.

Kohl also ensured that Baby, who passed away on December 26, 2012, had the time of her life as they trav- eled around the country to meet movers and shakers. Her goal of exposing this dog raised in a filthy cage in the dark to all the wonders of the wider world proved to be the most inspiring for our situation. While we were not able to spirit Freddie away on planes or place him in the arms of Barack Obama for a photo op, we managed to expand his world almost on a Baby scale, introducing him to many different places and faces that helped bring him out of himself and bring his ability to trust in alignment with his ability to love.

On the seventh anniversary of his adoption, after two years of upheaval and changes to both our lives, I wrote him a love letter.

September 11, 2017

It was seven years ago today, dear Freddie, that you came to us. As I sit here this morning in our Vancouver home, I look at you as you doze on the sunny balcony and try to imagine what you have made of these past tumultuous years.

After our home in Sidney was sold, you joined me part-time in my New Westminster flat, and then when Rudi came into my life and scooped me up, much as we did you in 2010, and I moved to the West End to join him, you also landed, cat-like, on your feet, taking life's changes as they came. The condo above the linden trees of Nelson Street became your new forever home, and Rudi your new alpha dad.

I often wonder, thinking back several Septembers ago, about how much you had traveled just to get to where we could find you. What do you remember of that day when the kind people from the BCSPCA Kamloops arrived to spring you from your prison? Do you ever think back to that long ride in the Drive for Lives van, surrounded by other dogs, among them your siblings, also freed from misery and hoping for happy homes or, at least, to find some certainty in a life characterized by flux and instability?

You rolled down from the Interior, up and down mountains, through valleys, finally reaching the sea and a ferry, where you sat in your travel crate for an hour and a half of gentle rocking, the motion that always seemed to soothe you on our future sailings with you. Surely the sights you saw after that were just as unforgettable—the shelter on Napier Lane, more kind people to look after you, the kennel you shared with Ichabod, and the day when two men arrived and stood outside the gate, saw you trembling there, and said, "He's the one."

Sweetheart, that was your Gotcha Day, and ours, too.

We never knew your actual birthday, because such records are not kept in the sort of place you had come from. So this day you joined our family became your true day of birth, and we the parents who gave you life in taking you into ours. That was our gift to you, as you became and continue to be the gift of all gifts to us.

How can we thank you for all you have given us, taught us, about what matters most in life? Courage, determination, trust, compassion—and many lessons that cannot be named or quantified, which take root and flower in the heart and soul, and make their presence known.

Your first dad and I taught a thin, terrified shelter dog how to trust. How to trust that the food in his bowl was his and would never be empty.

We taught that dog to play with toys he did not know what to do with at first. We bought him a soft bed to sleep on in our bedroom, and then, at his insistence that he was ready, we let him jump up between us, and we ended up repurposing the little bed to hold his ever increasing collection of toys which he learned were for chasing, throwing around, chewing, and sleeping on—ultimately, he would have five toy boxes scattered throughout the house, and would amaze his dads by learning not only to identify what we called his "pets" by sight but by name, digging down through the others to find Funky Monkey or Rainbow Lemur when we asked him to do so.

We taught that dog the joy of running like the wind, chasing his favorite green ball around the soccer field behind our house. After the way he had started, confined, separated from healthy stimuli, to see him fly around and the joy with which he did so was almost more than we could take; we had happy tears.

He learned that the wide spaces he feared were not a threat. This lesson stayed with him even on the day when he found himself chased by a larger dog that had entered the field, unnoticed.

You were terrified that day, as were we, our fear mixed with that crushing guilt that our poor judgment had exposed you to danger. You ran past us, still carrying your green ball, too fast for us to catch you. It was a scene I would replay in my mind over and over again as I wrote about Rags, dispatch dog of the American First Division in World War I, who fled over battle-ravaged ground, bullets and shrapnel flying over his ears, to carry a message to the men behind the earthworks and save the lives of countless soldiers who may never have known, when they died in their beds as grandfathers decades later, that they owed the second act of their lives to a little dog who refused to be scared by the horrors of human war.

Les and I headed off the larger dog, then we went searching frantically for you, fearing you had forgotten everything we had taught you, with good reason, as we had put you in a situation of danger and could not be trusted. We feared you had run blindly into the busy streets around our home, or even to the highway not far away, and that we would find you dead on the road, if we found you at all.

Yet, when we returned home, white with fear because we hadn't found you and not knowing what to do next, we spotted you sitting beside the back door, the last place we had thought to look. The pup that had never had a home till now knew where his home was, and still gave us his trust by believing that if he stayed there, though not knowing where we were, we would eventually come back and find you.

You showed us that, however many fears you still had about many aspects of the world, which in truth you had only started to come to know, you had a fierce love of your home. On one memorable occasion, you, all of fifteen pounds, angrily chased off a burglar from our garden, of whose presence we had been unaware, and on another occasion, you drove from our house an intruder who had crept in and got as far as up the stairs. When the police arrived, the man tried to tell them that our "fierce" dog had threatened him. There you sat, all black fluff and sharp nose and bright brown eyes, and the grinning cops knew who was telling the truth.

You also proved you had the chops to be a police service dog. I'll always remember the time you pulled us off your accustomed path home from our walk through downtown Sidney, that warm summer day, and strained at your harness to get us close enough to an SUV, windows rolled up tight, sitting there in the sun, from which we could hear the faint cries of a dog. We asked the restaurant nearby to page the owner of the car, and out came a woman making excuses for why she was eating in air-conditioned comfort while her dog was near death in a hot car.

You saved that pup's life that day.

And what about the time you zigzagged us down an alleyway and up to a trash can, where we saw a wooden donation box in the shape of a dog, its plexiglass belly shattered, donations gone. We recognized the box as being from a downtown Sidney animal charity, Animals for Life, and with you trotting alongside we brought it back to the shop, where the volunteers, who had been crying over the theft, now smiled to have their beloved donation box back in one piece. They cheered you, remember? And you got an extra special treat when we reached home.

You showed a compassion we had not suspected was in you, toward a human being you barely knew. When our friend Bob lay in his bed at hospice that last Christmas of his life, his normally cool, collected personality upended into sudden floods of tears from the hormone treatments he was taking for prostate cancer, his face broken every so often by pain that even the magic of modern science could not completely dull, you jumped up on his bed, unbidden, and nestled there in his lap. We moved to lift you off, knowing that is where all Bob's pain was concentrated. But you seemed to know that, too. And Bob, who had been weeping, was now calm, his hand on your head, his eyes closed like yours. "I'm in heaven," he whispered. Bob died the next day, but he took with him that memory of you, which you chose to give him.

In these past seven years, you traveled thousands of miles with us, visiting Yosemite National

Park, wading in the Merced River and posing atop Glacier Point; crossing the Golden Gate Bridge and strolling through Golden Gate Park; eating snow at Whistler and at Crater Lake, and playing on the sandy beaches of California, Oregon, Washington, and British Columbia. You met people from around the world: authors, politicians, conservationists, scholars, journalists, actors and artists of note, along with just plain folks, and all they could talk about was you and the privilege of having made your acquaintance. People who only knew you from social media would divert vacation plans and find reasons to visit Victoria and Vancouver for the chance of meeting you. Locally, you became so popular among the merchants of Sidney that you were chosen for inclusion in Bill Kierans's 2012 book *The Dogs of Sidney by the Sea*, proceeds of which went to the BCSPCA. It was wonderful to tell Bill the story of your rescue and how far you had come in just two years, and to see how many people in Sidney recognized you and were moved by your story, how grateful they were to meet you.

We took you to SAINTS (Senior Animals in Need Today Society) in Mission, to meet animals there who found refuge and love when there was no place else to go. Within moments of our arrival, as we stood at the fence, Emily, the black-and-white cow who had been rescued as a calf from a kill-pen, ran across the field, put her head through the wires, and in one swipe of her tongue took in your entire little body in a single kiss. Not only humans but animals love you at first sight. You put up with our entering you in BCSPCA calendar contests, posing you for the photos used in the calendars, allowing us to make a stamp from your paw with which to "pawtograph" your photos. You raised thousands of dollars over those years to help other animals in need, just as you were helped.

We did our best to teach you that a good life, a proper life, a life worth living, is not about fear but about love, and you taught us, too. When your first forever home became never more and your dads had to live apart, you showed us that love survives parting, even when the love that brought two people together is no longer there. At first, you pivoted between one home and another, but as you drew closer to your new dad, Rudi, it made much more sense for you to live with us in the West End. In so many ways, you told us you were ours, and we yours.

There, you adjusted to life in a city bigger than you had ever known, with its traffic and busyness and unavoidable meetings with the dogs you never could feel comfortable with, but who are always drawn to you as moth to flame. You loved our daily walks through the green depths of Stanley Park, where you became, unofficially, Sergeant Freddie of the Squirrel Admonishing Task Force. Those squirrels will be chattering down the generations about the little black monster in a duck-patterned raincoat who terrorized them from twenty feet below.

Elaine and Melissa, your beloved groomers on Davie Street, made you the cock of the walk; every six weeks, Rudi and I had the pleasure of walking newly-coiffed you home to Nelson Street, able to move only a few feet at a time as we were stopped by admiring passersby, to whom we always told your story—the Oliver Twist, as we called you, who finally found his rightful home. As Elaine liked to say, you were the most loved dog in all the West End.

It's been said that the attainment of seven years in a relationship marks a potential turning point—the "seven-year itch," when we humans may reassess who we're spending our lives with and whether we should continue to do so.

An itch means only one thing to you—something to scratch. As always, a much more sensible take on life. Perhaps the passage of seven years signals a very different turning point for animals than humans. The years from 2014 to 2016 comprised a two-year earthquake, every day shaking down another belief we thought we could always rely on. On the worst days, I sometimes thought it would be better not to survive. I did, though, in part through my writing, pouring into books about the animal–human condition, inspired by you, all that gave me pain and also all that gave me hope.

But I mostly stuck around for you. You kept me company through bleak days and nights, looking to me for security and giving me security in return. And reminding me of my promise to you seven years ago—to give you the happy life and love you deserve. Because of you, I decided life was worth it, that lesson we had hoped to teach you but which you already understood better than we knew and were able to teach us.

If the past seven years have taught me that we can never know just how a plot will unfold from how the story starts, you have been the constant bright light through darkness, the happiest choice I ever made, the greatest creative catalyst for me as writer.

Here's to seven more years, dear boy, and to the wonderful place called Now, where we can always find you and you can always be sure you will find us.

Always.

A Love Letter

PART TWO

CHAPTER SIX

New Life

OUR DIVORCE WOULD NOT be final till May 2016, but that spring our house in Sidney sold. I'd been offered a job near Vancouver and had found an apartment in New Westminster.

Les had helped me move furniture to my small flat, and Freddie seemed excited for me, running around the empty rooms, his nails clicking on the vintage hardwood floors. "I think he'll like being here," Les said, referring to our decision to split custody.

It was a nice idea, but it didn't work as we'd hoped. While the building manager had welcomed my having a dog, he then informed me that I should bring Freddie in by the back door and not attract too much attention. What further unnerved me was that, because my hours were long and unpredictable, I'd often come home to the flat to find Freddie in a state. I had noisy neighbors, Freddie was alone in a strange place, and the idea of him being there while I was away began to gnaw at me and adversely affect my performance on the job.

Finally, I had to ask Les to take him for longer periods while I figured out how to make this new life work. Thus began some months of what I can only describe as a slow-motion nervous breakdown. I was unable to keep the job that had brought me to the mainland. I started another in downtown Vancouver, which ultimately proved to me that a new job and mental distress are not compatible. I also had a book contract to fulfil, and I felt no joy in writing the promised book. The euphoria of having survived the constantly shifting setting of my once settled life, which had exploded like a landmine under my unwitting feet, was gone.

Then I met Rudi.

A designer who lived in a lofty condo among the treetops of the West End, Rudi took me into his life in a loving embrace that left more than enough room for Freddie. Having experienced, like me, the breakup of a relationship that included beloved dogs, Rudi understood what Freddie and I had been through and what we both needed to make it better. We shared so much already.

A fellow lover of dogs, mid-century design, and Harry Potter, Rudi also shared with me descent from a famous saint of medieval Germany, Elisabeth of Hungary (1207–1231). Through his father, a post–World War II refugee to Canada from the former Yugoslavia, where a German colony had been established in the eighteenth century, Rudi descended from Elisabeth's daughter, Sophie of Hesse, as do I through my German grandmother. Patron of the homeless and sick, Elisabeth of Hungary had sold all her valuables to fund a hospital in which she served as nurse, an admirable example by any standard. Another reason why I liked her was her admiration for and friendship with Francis of Assisi and her apparent love of animals, especially birds, who sang to her in her final hours. And having her as a shared ancestor also meant I could give Rudi a kitchen apron imprinted with Elisabeth's image—she is also patron saint of bakers—and know he'd not only get it but love it. (And it inspired him to do more baking, which was a plus for both Freddie and me.)

I asked Rudi recently what he remembers about the first time he met Freddie. He recalls the day that Les dropped Freddie off with me at the entrance to the Nelson Street building and I brought him up in the elevator. Freddie's nails clicked on the terracotta tiles of Rudi's entryway, and there stood Rudi, ready to welcome the new member of his family. Only Freddie, as on so many other occasions, didn't follow the sentimental script Rudi and I both had in mind. In fact, as Rudi remembers, Freddie walked around him and into the living room, looked at his surroundings, and peered out the glass door at the balcony. Then he gazed back at us wonderingly. Rudi told me later, "I thought, 'He'll warm to me,'" but I had my doubts. After all, Les had been and for some time still was Freddie's alpha dad. It might be that that situation was unchangeable. And whatever happened, we'd have to live with it. Was it any surprise, after all the strange changes to a once orderly life, that order we'd promised this dog after his beginnings in disorder, that Freddie might still be a bit skeptical about this new adventure?

I had started a new job downtown, which meant Rudi was with Freddie on his own. Rudi later told me that while I was at the office, late one afternoon, he was sitting on the sofa making notes for a meeting when Freddie jumped up and nestled beside him. As he had done that evening when I'd been shelving books, Freddie had decided this dad was probably OK after all. But while after that evening in 2010 Freddie simply came to accept me, in 2016 he had decided Rudi was his new alpha dad. "He was never far from my side after that day," Rudi said.

Over the years, my role as chief bottlewasher, meal prep coordinator, and bath attendant had only allowed a certain familiarity, but Freddie had always allowed Les to pick him up off the bed without snapping or fuss, or to take away a chew treat that was making him aggressive. Now Rudi had taken Les's place.

Lightning, happily, had struck the same place twice.

SINCE FIRST ARRIVING IN Victoria in 2005 and visiting the birthplace of Emily Carr, arguably Canada's greatest female painter (some would argue our greatest of either sex), I had been intrigued by her love of animals. They had provided her the kind of solace they had given me in my own troubled youth. The summer I turned nine, when my mother was so ill that she had to be hospitalized, my father was unable to look after all three of us and so we went by twos to stay across town in our paternal grandparents' seven-gabled house.

During our time there, our grandmother, Gertrude, devised projects to keep us stimulated and our minds off our mother's situation. We were often busy at the broad surface of the dining table, making dogs out of yarn and coat hangers, doing macramé and découpage stuff. I remember one of those projects quite well. Grandma gave me a stack of vintage women's magazines going back to the 1940s and suggested I clip from them pictures I liked and to group them in page protectors snapped into a three-ring binder.

I still have the binder I made that day, and it's interesting to see that everything I carefully cut out features an animal, most of them dogs and cats (with the exception of an image of kilted children dancing a highland fling). I think Grandma knew that while we missed our mother, we also missed our pets at home. Though our father looked after them that summer, at our grandparents' house I often cried after we'd gone to bed, worrying about them worrying about us.

It was a consolation to have two dogs in the house—a Chinese pug called Cindy and her King Charles Spaniel son, Scooter, the product of a mésalliance made possible by a hole in the backyard fence. These little dogs followed us everywhere, running with us through the fields around the house, sitting obediently nearby as we helped Gertrude feed the elderly jenny next door, along with the pups brought to the front garden by their stray mother and the semi-feral cats that she gave milk and cat chow to each morning on the porch. It was at my grandparents' house that I found old books about animals, with vividly colored illustrations, including some volumes that had belonged to my father and his twin brother from their childhood in the 1930s. I still have some of them, in addition to the books I found on my own: *Black Beauty, Old Yeller, The Red Pony, Donkey's Glory*.

These animals, real and in pictures and in words, grounded my constantly shifting world, at least for a while, and gave me a place to escape to when life became too difficult to cope with. I knew they had done the same for Emily Carr. She had had a menagerie that rivaled ours—dogs, cats, mice, birds, squirrels—and a Javanese macaque she called Woo, after the sound the little female made. Carr had purchased Woo from a pet shop in downtown Victoria, rescuing her from the older and larger monkeys who were picking on her, and likely seeing something of herself in the runt, youngest of a family in which she was considered the outsider and did nothing to disabuse her proper sisters of that opinion.

I believed Woo played a role in Carr's life that was more than that of the many rescues Carr was known for keeping. I think she kept Woo for reasons beyond adding an animal to her menagerie that she did not already have (monkeys, which should never be kept as pets, are notoriously more rambunctious and destructive than your average human toddler in the throes of the terrible twos). To me, it seemed that Carr's technique and her clarity of vision as an artist went up several notches, became freer, looser in form and conception, only after a monkey joined her in her studio, and I thought there might be enough to write a book.

The curator of Carr House, Jan Ross, encouraged me to do so, as did my godfather, the playwright William Luce, who with his muse, the actress Julie Harris, had been gathering material over the years for plays based on Carr's life. Other projects under contract took precedence, however, and then life itself got in the way, and by the time the idea came to me again, it was on a walk with Rudi and Freddie in Stanley Park.

Freddie loved these walks. He seemed to become more himself, more the bold, bright little dog we knew was always in there, keen to explore and even more keen to put the many squirrels of the park in their place. He had an especial attraction to the steep area of lawn where the rose garden is located, just above Pipeline Road, and so we navigated to that area quite frequently. In reading a history of Stanley Park, established in 1888,

I discovered that there had been a zoo in the grounds of the park as late as the 1990s, and part of that zoo had included, in various iterations, a Monkey House. And that's when I made the connection: This pleasant stretch of grass and roses, all fragrance and brilliant colors, was the location of the Monkey House, and thus the place where Woo had spent her final year of life.

In the winter of 1937, after suffering a heart attack and being hospitalized, Emily Carr was convinced by her doctor and family to surrender most of the animals she had in her home, since it was believed, naturally enough, that in her condition she couldn't care for them. Homes were easily found for the birds, mice, cats, and griffon dogs. But nobody wanted Woo. A small but feisty macaque, Woo had lived in Carr's home for over a decade, wearing clothes to protect her against the winter cold, eating what Carr ate, accompanying Carr on her local peregrinations to sites where she could set up camp and paint away from the madding crowds. It is doubtful Woo even saw herself as a monkey, as her unhappy meetings with other monkeys in Victoria seemed to prove.

In despair and not knowing what else to do that cold winter of 1937, Carr wrote to the keeper of the Monkey House, asking him if he would take Woo, and he did. Woo was nailed into a crate in James Bay, shipped across the strait and, because she was afraid of the other monkeys, placed in a cage by herself, though exposed, like the other monkeys, to the public. And that is where Woo died a year later, having never seen Carr again.

Rudi, Freddie, and I returned to the site again and again, as I tried to understand what that last year might have been like for Woo. With all my biographical subjects, I like to visit their graves, if extant. This site felt as close to a grave as Woo would ever have. But I decided I also needed to find the last resting place of Carr, to see if something came to mind that would help me decide to write the life of her monkey. I had written the life of Rags of the First Division and tried to get inside the heads of war horses in my biography of Dorothy Brooke. But I wasn't sure about Woo.

Maybe I needed Carr's blessing.

At Easter in 2017, Rudi, Freddie, and I sailed to Vancouver Island to see family. We had time for that visit to Carr's grave in Victoria that I had been pondering for so long. She is buried in Ross Bay Cemetery, the last resting place of many of Victoria's pioneer families. All I knew was that Carr lay in the family plot, but the map I'd brought with me was unclear. I confess my bearings were also thrown off by the fact I was looking at the map with just one eye, the other peeled for bylaw officers, because I knew we were breaking a Victoria bylaw by bringing Freddie into the burial grounds.

Freddie had had an interesting history with cemeteries. We took him to graveyards where we searched for specific plots and markers, and he had an uncanny ability to guide us. My friend Dan and I once took Freddie to a cemetery outside Vancouver, to place incense and flowers on the grave of Dan's grandfather. It was raining and windy, and the weather and light played tricks with Dan's memory, so we wandered a bit, searching for the site. Then Freddie pulled us toward a series of gravestones, and I read the name on one of them. "See, it's him!"

Years earlier, Freddie had done the same in Grants Pass, Oregon. In 1864, a maternal relative, Benjamin Baird, had died there after meeting a grizzly bear in the woods and had been buried in the local cemetery under a white marble headstone. Vandalism prompted the community to move the remaining stones to Croxton Memorial Park, where they were set into a concrete circle planted with flowers. Les and I walked around the circle more than once, looking for the stone that stated that the man had been killed by a bear, but could not find it. We were headed to the car when Freddie, whose leash I'd been holding, pulled me back to the circle and jumped up on the fieldstone ledge around it. There, under one of his paws, was Baird's stone. The look in his eyes said, "Why didn't you just ask me?"

It didn't take Freddie long to find the Carr family plot, or Carr's stone, a simple rectangle, tiny as a calling card compared to the outsized dimensions of Carr's wild life. Freddie sat on her grave for a long time. Slowly, my fear of a bylaw officer running at us with an admonitory forefinger in the air dissipated, replaced by baffled incredulity. We simply stood there, as the wind bent the trees.

A LITTLE OVER TWO years later, I sat at a signing table at Bolen Books, across the street from our condo in Oaklands, inscribing copies of my biography of Woo, which had just been published by Douglas & McIntyre. Rudi was there with Freddie on his lap, the tartan jacket of the latter echoed in the bowtie of the former. The crowd was larger than I had expected.

In the front row was Dr. Sylvia van Kirk, a retired University of Toronto professor and author who for several years had tried to catch my interest with an idea for a book about Muggins, the fundraising spitz of World War I–era Victoria. I was rather embarrassed to see her because I had not proved very cooperative. Sylvia had researched Muggins, who lived between 1913 and 1920, for several years, seeking out elderly people who might remember him, unearthing clippings and photos about his three-year career raising the modern equivalent of $250,000 for war-related charities. She also found hints as to what might have happened to his body, preserved by a Victoria taxidermist in 1920 and later used to raise funds for charities during the Second World War, before it vanished without a trace.

Sylvia had given talks about Muggins, and she knew everything there was to know about him. But she wanted a co-author to help her put a book together. And when she came to a book signing for my Rags biography, hosted at Tanner's Books in Sidney, she presented her copy for my signature, and that's when she broached the subject. I said it sounded interesting, but I was then about to depart for the mainland and a new life there. She contacted me again, after I moved to New Westminster, and again when I was living with Rudi in Vancouver. I finally emailed her that, unfortunately, I was not a good co-anything, and could not see myself working in tandem with anyone on a book.

In addition to my contracted book projects, I had on the front burner what I believed would be my best book about an animal, a full-length, factual biography of Flush (1841–1854), the spaniel companion of Elizabeth Barrett Browning, famously given a fictional biography by the novelist Virginia Woolf in 1933. I had much to say about Flush and his world and his influence down the ages. I had wandered London the year before, thinking about Flush and Barrett Browning. I thought about the rural servant Ben Embery, from whom Flush had been taken to be given to the young author; the servant

Elizabeth Wilson, who looked after him the most; Flush's immortality gained through the published letters of Elizabeth and Robert Browning and their friends; and the production in 1933 of Rudolf Besier's play, *The Barretts of Wimpole Street*, which gave Woolf the idea for her book.

There were certain similarities between Flush and Freddie. Both had come out of rural beginnings to become the muses of writers in urban settings, both had been through numerous household moves and adventures, and both had had to adjust to new dads (Robert Browning in Flush's case, Rudi in Freddie's), with whom they fell in love after a standoffish beginning. Flush had had a skin condition that caused hair loss, echoing Freddie's persistent alopecia. And, just as Flush had come into Barrett Browning's life to bring her happiness after her years of poor health and the tragic death of her favorite brother, Freddie had brought joy and inspiration to mine, sitting beside my desk as I wrote, just as Flush sat on Barrett Browning's sofa as she composed.

And there was something else. I had only once written about a topic that had already been covered by another author. In 1930, Jack Rohan had published a life of Rags of the First Division, written for young adults. A successful and well-written book, *Rags, the Story of a Dog Who Went to War* contained a great deal of information on Rags that Rohan had picked up from surviving military officers and men, but a good deal of it was fictionalized and sensationalized, material that could not be matched to facts. It had been out of print for decades. I had discovered more information about the second half of Rags's life, and all together, a new biography was mandated. But writing about an animal like Muggins, whose life had already been researched by someone else, about whom I knew nothing, whose existence hadn't stirred me to search for more, just didn't sit right with me. I felt I might not be able to capture, conjure, and celebrate the dog in the way he evidently deserved. (Of course, as with Rags, there was a wealth of material on Muggins that had yet to be tapped, but I didn't know that then.)

So my face went red when Sylvia approached me on this occasion with a copy of *Woo* in her hands. Beside me stood Rudi, holding Freddie on his leash, so that people could see with their own eyes the famous canine muse in person. I inscribed Sylvia's book, then handed it to her with thanks, but she wasn't looking at me. She was looking fondly at Freddie, dancing around in his tartan coat. She smiled at me then, took the book, and said, "I think I knew this when I heard you tonight. But now, seeing your Freddie, I know it. You are the one to write about Muggins." She asked me if she could come see me the following week, to share her years of documents with me.

I AM OFTEN ASKED why I dedicate my books "to Freddie." "Because he was always there," I reply, quoting novelist Edith Wharton's now classic comment about her little dog: he was "the heartbeat at my feet."

This is true. Freddie often lay on the round Chinese carpet in my office as I ploughed through source materials, lifting his head with interest at my "aha!" moments, getting up to come see what was wrong when I put my face in my hands and groaned that I should never have started a book, what was I thinking,

I should never have become a writer, et cetera. Freddie was often with me when I lay atop the bedcovers to read and study and make notes. Where galleys were concerned, he had a mysterious but charming habit of licking the page I happened to be working on, so that every so often a sheet would end up with a smear of red ink across the margin.

This book about Muggins felt different from what I had written before, more personal and alive. I was writing about a spitz and I lived with a spitz, whose character I had been studying by then for nine years. It almost felt as if Freddie was helping me resurrect his white doppelgänger, who had vanished and yet left his imprint on lives his fundraising had saved, in wars no animal ever caused, in a community that still remembered him.

It meant postponing my Flush biography again. But this was a chance, I knew, to make Freddie part of a book in ways that I had never been able to do before and might not be able to do again. So when Sylvia came by our house for tea, served in my grandmother's Spode cups, Freddie greeting her as he only did ladies of a certain age, we agreed that I would assume the mantle of Muggins's historian.

I began reviewing all the files and photographs, letting the book take shape in my mind, with Freddie at my feet or beside me on the bed. As we walked through downtown Victoria, timing how long it would take for a spitz like Muggins to carry his tins full of coins from the Inner Harbour to Canadian Red Cross HQ downtown; as I mused about what it must have been like when Muggins was saluted by the Prince of Wales at the Queen Victoria memorial in September 1919, I could not have guessed in a million years how important this book would be not just for Muggins or for me, but especially for Freddie.

↑ My paternal grandmother Gertrude Launspach Menzies (*left*) and friend in 1914 Los Angeles, holding puppies of Gertrude's beloved Boston terrier. Gertrude had a gift for charming animals, wild or domestic, and had an especial fondness for dogs. GRANT HAYTER-MENZIES COLLECTION

↓ The goofy effigy dog on the grave of Gertrude's ancestor Tamburga von Hutten, 1354—one of many little dogs in my grandmother's family history. Hutten family chapel, Schlüchtern, Hessen. OTTO VOLK, MARBURG

↑ My maternal grandmother, Nina Lewis Strawser (*left*), and sister Vera with the farm dog Joe, who saved their toddler sister from drowning. When the elderly Joe disappeared one night from the farm, Nina forever wondered what had happened to him, assuming he had departed to save his human family from seeing his sufferings. GRANT HAYTER-MENZIES COLLECTION

↓ Freddie's first photograph in his new home, September 11, 2010. For the first hour, he sat in a corner, his head down, and shook. LES HAYTER

→ Freddie with my godfather, the playwright William Luce, in March 2011 in Sidney, BC. "He's our little Oliver Twist," Bill said, "who has found his rightful family at last."
LES HAYTER

↓ Freddie at Glacier Point, Yosemite National Park, in September 2011.
LES HAYTER

← Freddie and I in Japantown, San Francisco, CA, 2013. LES HAYTER

↓ My first author photo that included Freddie, used on the dustjacket of one of my books. A 1930 photograph of Rags, subject of my first book inspired by Freddie, stands on the chest behind us. DEVON MACKENZIE

→ Freddie and Rudi at our first picnic together in Stanley Park, Vancouver, BC, 2016. GRANT HAYTER-MENZIES

↓ Selfie with Freddie and *New York Times* bestselling dog author Maria Goodavage in Vancouver, BC, 2017. GRANT HAYTER-MENZIES

↑ Freddie with me at Tanner's Books in Sidney, BC, in 2018. On the table were two of the books Freddie inspired, waiting to be signed.
RUDI KLAUSERYTER

↓ Freddie with Rudi at Emily Carr House in Victoria, BC, 2018.
GRANT HAYTER-MENZIES

↑ At the grave of Emily Carr, Ross Bay Cemetery, in Victoria, BC, Good Friday 2017. GRANT HAYTER-MENZIES

→ Freddie's third and last BCSPCA calendar contest photo, appearing in the March 2021 calendar. Over the course of his life, Freddie raised thousands for animal shelters through calendar contests like these and through royalties donated from books he inspired. GRANT HAYTER-MENZIES

↑ Helping the author unbox copies of *Woo, The Monkey Who Inspired Emily Carr: A Biography* (Douglas & McIntyre) in 2019. In all, he helped unbox author's copies for seven books. GRANT HAYTER-MENZIES

↓ With Rudi and I at the Butchart Gardens, 2017. Freddie was a favourite of fellow visitors for some ten years. GRANT HAYTER-MENZIES

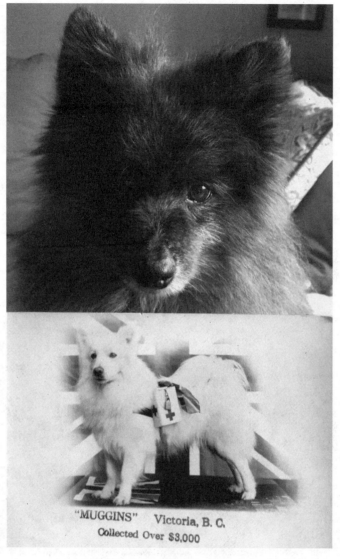

"MUGGINS" Victoria, B. C.
Collected Over $3,000

↑ Freddie with a 1917 postcard of Muggins, the famed fundraising dog of World War I–era Victoria, during research for *Muggins: The Life and Afterlife of a Canadian Canine War Hero* (Heritage House, 2021). GRANT HAYTER-MENZIES

↑ Freddie's last Christmas, December 2020, in Victoria, BC. Every year, we photographed him sitting on a crazy quilt made by my great-grandmother for my toddler father, pieced from my great-grandfather's silk cravats. GRANT HAYTER-MENZIES

↑ A photograph of Freddie five days before his death, in Sidney, BC, on October 20, 2021, with flowers sent by the BCSPCA main office in Vancouver. He was present for the unboxing of *Muggins: The Life and Afterlife of a Canadian Canine War Hero*, in which he appears as my companion on research jaunts around Victoria, and for the first Zoom launch of the book. GRANT HAYTER-MENZIES

↓ Freddie in Stanley Park in 2017, keeping the squirrels in order. GRANT HAYTER-MENZIES

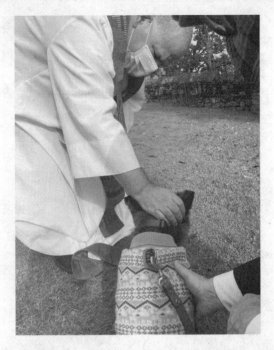

↑Freddie's last blessing, October 4, 2020, from Rev. Daniel Fournier, at a Blessing of the Animals on St. Francis Day, St. Luke's Anglican Church, Victoria, BC. GRANT HAYTER-MENZIES

↓ Freddie with his certificate of graduation from his course of three months of chemotherapy from Boundary Bay Veterinary Specialty Hospital, November 2020. GRANT HAYTER-MENZIES

↑ Rudi and Freddie, Centennial Beach, September 2021, at the start of his second course of chemotherapy. GRANT HAYTER-MENZIES

← Freddie waiting at the garden door of our Sidney home for Rudi to return from his COVID-19 vaccine appointment. He stood there for over an hour, watching for his return.
GRANT HAYTER-MENZIES

↓ Oil portrait of Freddie, by artist Vicky Bowes, 2014.
GRANT HAYTER-MENZIES

CHAPTER SEVEN

Cancer Journey

BEING INVITED TO TALK about my biography of Woo at
the Vancouver Institute in March 2020 was even
more of an honor than I realized. With two more speak-
ers scheduled to fill out the season, COVID-19 lockdown
descended on much of our world in British Columbia
and elsewhere, making my gig the last one till restric-
tions eased the following year.

Up to that point, the strange virus making its way
through families, neighborhoods, cities, and nations had
not had much of an effect on our household. At my day
job with a local charity, we were required to adopt a host
of sanitation practices, to keep distance to a maximum,
and so on. Then the situation became exponentially
more troubling for everyone, and when it was decided
that our organization couldn't function under these
conditions, the doors were closed.

I was concerned, of course, since that job had been
my primary source of income, aside from a few royalties, but it was a relief to be able to rely on government
help under these extraordinary circumstances affecting

- 96 -

everyone's lives. I had a bit of a cushion, if only at that point in theory. Bill Luce, my godfather, had died in December 2019, leaving me a bequest as well as making me executor of his literary estate, and in those days before all theatres were shuttered, some royalties were still coming in for him as well, now funneled to me.[1] Once the cash inheritance came through, thought to occur in June or July, I'd conceivably have something to fall back on when government subsidies for those whose employment had been affected by the pandemic expired. But when that would come and of what it would consist, I still didn't know, and that uncertainty, mixed with gratefulness that I had a legacy to contemplate at all, added to the tensions we all had to cope with and hopes we didn't dare indulge in.

In the meantime, I was working on my Muggins project. While Sylvia van Kirk had handed me an important archive of materials on which to base my book, I began to find other information, including potential clues as to how this purebred spitz came to Victoria, where he'd come from (a millionaire's mansion in Calgary), and more details on the people who cared for him during his short, eventful life. And, of course, I was adding to my stash of materials for my planned biography of Flush, which now filled a bookshelf floor to ceiling, with more materials obtained electronically and stored on my hard drive. Even in the thick of what became *Muggins: The Life and Afterlife of a Canadian Canine War Hero*, I had one eye on Flush, and was even sketching out scenarios for how to shape the book.

Since winter, Freddie had been experiencing a recurrent cough. It seemed to happen most when he drank water too fast, and we discouraged this by getting him

FREDDIE

to go at it more slowly, which seemed to help somewhat. All his life with us, Freddie had had the curse of Pomeranians—the reverse sneeze—and combined with the cough, we thought they might be related. But when the cough predominated, I contacted his vet, whose clinic was a few blocks over from us on Shakespeare Street.

Dr. Kelli Mulley was by then only seeing patients remotely for non-critical cases, and we had a few Zoom meetings where I presented Freddie's tongue, eyes, belly, et cetera, to my webcam, much to Freddie's bafflement. She believed it might be related to his trachea (another area where Pomeranians can have trouble), and on her advice we started using a little platform for his water bowl, so he didn't have to bend over to drink, as well as feeding him on the bed.

One of the hangovers from Freddie's earlier fearful days was that anything that startled him in the room where his food bowl normally sat made him shy away from eating there. We developed a routine, whenever a neighbor overhead was unremittingly noisy or when something had unexpectedly fallen to the floor in our living room or kitchen, of feeding him wherever he felt safe—a moving feast, as it were. This seemed to help where eating was concerned. But the coughing continued and seemed to be worsening. At last, we managed to get Freddie in to see Dr. Mulley in person. She had set up her clinic in a scheme we were to see a lot of that year: guardians handed over their pet to a veterinary technician at the door, then sat in their car or on a bench nearby, awaiting a phone call from the vet, and then the pet was handed back at the door. On this particular day, Rudi and I waited on folding chairs in a shady spot of the clinic's parking lot.

Freddie was no stranger to veterinary clinics. He found himself on a vet's examination table every year since 2013, when a short haircut, given against our wishes, triggered alopecia that never went away, followed by issues with his digestion and urinary tract requiring frequent checkups. The frequency did not make the experiences any easier for him; his earliest experience of being put under for a medical procedure was when he was neutered right after his rescue, when the whole world was an unknown quantity and he was afraid of everything. He clearly associated any subsequent visits with those episodes. Making things worse was the fact that, because of social distancing protocols, we now could not accompany him into the exam room.

On that visit, Dr. Mulley diagnosed a heart murmur, one that was rather serious—a Stage Three or Four. The technical term for this condition is mitral valve disease, where a faulty valve causes turbulent blood flow in the heart. Dr. Mulley set Freddie up for an ultrasound, scheduled for July 14, to determine the details of his condition. The date caught my attention, for obvious reasons: On that day, in 1997, I had undergone surgery for thyroid cancer.

Come the day, we brought Freddie back to the clinic, where Dr. Mulley was joined by a specialist to do the ultrasound. Handing him over to a veterinary technician, we watched him go in and then took our seats on the folding chairs.

About thirty minutes later, my phone rang. I thought again of that summer of my cancer surgery, because when I answered, Dr. Mulley had that guarded tone I had heard from my own doctor in Portland over two decades before, when he phoned to tell me the results of my biopsy.

"While doing the ultrasound on his chest," Dr. Mulley told Rudi and me over speakerphone, "I decided to go further down into his abdomen. I'm sorry to tell you we found three lesions on his spleen. I believe he has hemangiosarcoma."

I remembered the last time Freddie had had a full body X-ray. It was part of a routine exam three years earlier by his Vancouver vet, Dr. Helene Childs. I had stood in Dr. Childs's exam room looking at the X-ray slide she placed against the light panel, and though I heard her tell me that everything was fine, what moved me was seeing Freddie's interior self—bones, organs, and all the substructure beneath his fluffy outer self— laid bare to the eye. I was particularly touched by the sight of Freddie's heart, which I felt beating against my chest or hand every day, the heart that I'd felt pound in fear or excitement or quietly matching the rhythm of his breath when he slept. Dr. Childs saw my wet eyes and touched my shoulder reassuringly. "They are just little miracles, inside and out," she said. "Aren't they?"

What a difference between that day and this. Hemangiosarcoma is one of the most aggressive cancers a canine can have, Dr. Mulley explained to us. It is a vascular cancer, meaning it develops in veins and vei- nous organs of the body, and can spread as fast as that suggests. It is fatal, with some patients living longer than others depending on therapies used—chemotherapy being at the top of the list. Even then, life might only be extended for another few months.

If we did nothing, we risked a tumor rupturing. When this happened, a dog basically bled to death. But chemo- therapy would be hard on an older dog with mitral valve disease: he might not survive surgery. Rock and a hard place.

I won't try to compare this to my own reaction to receiving news, years earlier, of my cancer diagnosis. In all but the most extraordinary circumstances, a human has options to draw on in these moments. He or she can call a relative, or a friend, draw on their faith, plunge into a Beethoven symphony, sob uncontrollably on the floor. Even to this day, what makes Freddie's cancer diagnosis most heart-rending is that he was unaware of the seriousness of the situation. He'd been unable to tell us about his condition, if he had any symptoms at all. Sheer dumb luck had led us to this moment, and had it led us too late?

That afternoon, on our short walk home, Freddie having recovered from his light sedation, we looked at his bouncy enthusiasm for the squirrels met along the way and both agreed: the worst of this was being unable to tell him how sick he was and being unwilling to show in his presence how devastated we were. This is when we began to cry mornings in the shower. Counterbalancing the incredulity and despair that blanketed us both, Rudi and I also had to buckle on our resolve. Dr. Mulley said that the sooner we got Freddie into surgery, the better for him, and he was set up with an appointment in two weeks with a specialist at WAVES (Westcoast Animal Veterinary Emergency Specialty Hospital), in Langford, just west of Victoria. In the interim, she started Freddie on heart medication that would provide him some protection from any deleterious cardiac issues that might arise during surgery.

The next two weeks were divvied up between two areas of fear: that we had to wait fourteen days to get him examined by the specialist, and that he might not survive the surgery that he needed if he was to have any hope of living.

When the day came—July 29, 2020—we drove Freddie out to WAVES and handed him over to the veterinary technician. "We'll call you once he's been seen by Dr. Branter," we were told.

To take some of the stress off, we walked across the parking lot to a Canadian Tire store. We were looking blindly at some summer patio furniture when my phone rang. It was Dr. Erinne Branter. An examination had made the picture very clear: Freddie had hemangiosarcoma and if he was to survive, the spleen and any other affected tissue had to come out right now. "You're in luck," she said. "There's been a cancellation this morning. Dr. Bolliger can take him this afternoon. We just need your OK." I gave it and we were told that as there might not be news for hours, and that Freddie was in the best hands possible, we should do ourselves the favour of going home, getting rest, and waiting for another call.

By 2020, Freddie had become something of a star among my many Facebook friends around the world. I had announced the diagnosis earlier in the month, which had prompted a response that moved and inspired us. Now I sat down to tell people, almost as if writing about another dog, the latest, and asked those who would or could to keep good thoughts for him as he underwent surgery. Hundreds of kind wishes came in, to the point where I couldn't read them all or respond.

One, though, stood out. Dr. Julia Bolton Holloway, a UK-born nun and scholar based in Florence, had helped me enormously in my Flush research, not least because she is guardian of the English cemetery in Florence where Elizabeth Barrett Browning was buried in 1861, seven years after the death of Flush. On hearing the news about Freddie, Julia told me she would gladly pray for him, and she did something else. Taking a first edition volume of Virginia Woolf's *Flush: A Biography*, Julia placed the book atop Barrett Browning's white marble tomb and, her hand on its cover, asked the universe to bless Freddie.

It was clear to me now that there would be no Flush biography from me. (Indeed, I wondered if I should abandon unfinished *Muggins*.) But that and everything else that had mattered to me did so no longer.

We had no idea what the future held—whether Freddie would survive the surgery or, having survived it, whether it would be enough to give him more time or, having started chemotherapy, whether treatment would agree with him and help him. But the most important job of my life had just been given to me: to help our dog fight the greatest battle that he had ever faced, the greatest one that had ever been stared down by the animals of war I had written about.

Making the responsibility immeasurably easier was the envelope that arrived in the mail right in the middle of this storm. It was the bequest from Bill. It proved sufficient to not only cover any costs for Freddie's treatment (we had excellent pet insurance, but one had to pay up front before being reimbursed: Freddie's care, from 2020–21, was to cost in total around $50,000 Canadian), with no need to worry about expense, but also to allow me to not worry for a time about work and to stay home to help care for Freddie for as long as it might take.

It was at this time I began a diary. I had been keeping journals since my teens, but this was different. This was to be a record of Freddie's health issues, treatment, and anything that needed setting down on paper about his cancer journey. Nobody in a position to know gave us hope of his having more than a few months of life, but I was determined to record his days and hours. Dr. Childs had said, after all, "They are little miracles, inside and out, aren't they?" That he was, cancer or no.

– Freddie Diary 2020 –

JULY 31

We had a call from Dr. Branter at WAVES in Langford: Freddie is ready to come home! "He is a very sensitive little dog," she said. After these two days of waiting for him to recover, so far away from us, we are grateful beyond belief. At home, we installed him on the bed. He's got a stapled incision up his belly. The cone we got for him last week seems too heavy, so I drove around to various pet supply stores till I found a nice light one. He still hates it, and we don't blame him. But he is resting most of the time, thank goodness.

AUGUST 3

I gave Freddie his last morphine capsule. After being uninterested in food for at least the past several weeks, he's now ravenous. It's as if getting rid of his diseased spleen has given him not just a chance to live but a chance to enjoy food as he did before. He continues to do well on his heart medication. There is no coughing.

AUGUST 10

We took Freddie to WAVES for follow-up and later his surgeon, Dr. Christian Bolliger, came out to talk to us. Freddie's spleen was in bad shape, barely functioning; seems to have been the only organ where cancer was present. We talked a bit about life expectancy and the

– 104 –

pros and cons of chemotherapy. We had already decided to move forward with it, so Dr. Bolliger made the referral to Boundary Bay Veterinary Specialty Hospital in Langley, on the mainland. We don't know what will happen next, but we have to try everything.

I don't want any regrets.

AUGUST 13

Took the ferry over to mainland—we've decided it makes more sense, given erratic sailing schedules, to stay there the night before Freddie's chemotherapy treatments, and is easier on him also. It also gave us a chance to walk him in Stanley Park! Hard to believe, watching him try to dash after squirrels, who seemed startled to see the monster of prior years returned to their patch, that he was on an operating table two weeks ago. We tried to get him to take it easy, but it is a joy to see him so full of life.

AUGUST 14

We couldn't go into the hospital with Freddie because of social distancing protocols, so after handing him over to his oncologist, Dr. Chamisa Herrera, we sat in the car in the parking lot, alongside lots of other people waiting for news about their pets.

A young man was parked beside us. He looked like he might be a tradesman, busy in the building boom erupting throughout the province even during the pandemic. He had that antsy appearance of somebody who has taken time off and can't escape looking at the clock. As he sat in the cab of his truck, he made calls on his cell phone and it was hard not to hear that they were mostly about the dog that had just been carried into the hospital. She was large, elderly, and ill, unable to walk.

FREDDIE

At one point, a veterinary tech came out to confer with the young man. "The procedure may be the only way we can extend her life," I heard her say. "Unfortunately, it will cost . . . ," and the amount was high, obviously impossibly high for the young man to afford. He continued to sit there after she left, staring straight ahead. Then he made some more calls, rested his head on the steering wheel, and sobbed.

Rudi and I couldn't look at each other.

We were relieved to be called and told that Freddie had aced his first chemotherapy induction with flying colors and was ready to go. At the gate outside the cancer clinic door, he got so excited to see us he wedged himself between the bars and it took all three of us, Rudi, the vet tech, and me, to get him out. We were given anti-nausea meds in case he needed them.

Dr. Herrera was very pleased. "He's a gracious boy," she told us over the phone.

Now, we wait and watch. And count our blessings.

AUGUST 15

Drove up to Sidney to get turkey tail mushroom, a natural immunity booster, and red krill oil from our friend Monica Mayse at Reigning Cats and Dogs. She has lots of it left from her sweet Aidan, who died two weeks ago from hemangiosarcoma. She swears it added years to his life. We have known her almost since the first day we brought Freddie home. She loves him and has such good advice. I thought about this the other day. With my parents and Bill gone, there is nobody we can lean on, except each other, and there are days I go down to see Monica just to lean on her for myself. She shares my late mother's cold fury toward people who abuse animals, and sometimes we get so furious together we end up laughing. It helps.

AUGUST 26

We celebrated Freddie's tenth Gotcha Day with just us and Rudi's sisters and brother-in-law. At the dollar store, I found those inflatable letters spelling "Happy Birthday" and strung them in the living room, along with purple and pink and blue bunting and balloons. Got a lovely shot of Freddie on the sofa with Rudi, looking happily up at all the decorations. He was in fine form and interested in all his biscuits, new toys and lovely cards, and the iced cookie for his birthday treat.

Tried not to think of the swift passage of time, of sands in an hourglass and ticking clocks.

Tried to think of all the reasons to be grateful.

AUGUST 27

We planned to take Freddie for a walk in Beacon Hill Park but news of a man with a gun being seen there, along with tents popping up in the park, put paid to that idea. We hope there will be a chance to take him again without fearing for safety. We don't know how long he has, do we? I have worked in some form of social service most of my working life—my mother was hounded by mental illness. I have sympathy for the sufferers. But my dog is living on borrowed time. Not being able to drive him to the park and walk him without fear of used needles or assurance of safe circumstances frustrates us.

SEPTEMBER 4

Freddie's second chemotherapy induction today in Langley.

We caught an early sailing and so were able to walk him in Stanley Park. He so loves it and it is so good for him, and for us. (And no men carrying guns.)

Freddie's appointment went well. Dr. Herrera says when she sees him in October, she will run an echocardiogram, as the doxorubicin being used is one of the toughest chemotherapies there is and can be hard on the heart. Thank goodness we started him on his heart meds in July.

He came out of the hospital all frisky and ready to go home. His next date is 24 September.

SEPTEMBER 11

It has been ten years today since we adopted Freddie at the Napier Lane BCSPCA. We drove him out to Sidney to see his old hometown. Monica was thrilled to see him again, as were other business owners up and down Beacon Avenue, who know him from years back. We bought him a jumper with squirrels on it. The trip tired him and he slept when we got back to Victoria.

SEPTEMBER 17

Took Freddie in for checkup with Dr. Mulley. She is delighted by his strength and energy, as we were at her reaction to how well he looks.

SEPTEMBER 24

Early ferry today. We are staying in a different hotel to see if we can find one where there is no noise during the night, because Freddie needs as much rest as he can get, and it's again not looking promising.

COVID-19 has made everything difficult.

Freddie was happy to walk in Stanley Park again, as were we. If only we could do this more often and under

Cancer Journey

different circumstances in Victoria. Trying to only show him smiles this trip.

Freddie's third chemotherapy induction today.

And I was in a traffic accident this morning.

There was a terrific downpour. I left the hotel, after a sleepless night worried about everything, to find a cheap microwave oven to heat Freddie's breakfast, as none was provided in the room.

I wasn't thinking and am thankful the crash wasn't worse for the other driver or for me, and especially that neither Freddie nor Rudi were with me when it happened.

We had to take a taxi to the hospital for Freddie's appointment, then I found I'd mistakenly written down a time that made us an hour early.

We tried to keep our stress to an absolute minimum so that it does not splash over onto Freddie. He's his usual happy self, a bit anxious as he knows what's coming in the clinic.

I'm having some strange stomach issues, but who wouldn't?

Freddie aced his treatment again and there is hope, for which I am profoundly grateful.

SEPTEMBER 26

My heart pounding, balance off, but glad to be home and that Freddie did well yesterday. Two more chemo treatments to go! Taking him for his evening walk later, we stopped, gobsmacked, to see a full rainbow. What did Charlotte Brontë call it? A "bow of promise." Please let it be so.

FREDDIE

OCTOBER 4, FEAST OF ST. FRANCIS

We took Freddie up the hill to a Blessing of the Animals ceremony at St. Luke's Anglican above Oaklands.

This was his third Blessing. His first time was when we were living in Vancouver. We sat with him in a pew in St. Andrew's and sang a lovely hymn with the congregation, accompanied by happy barking, meows, and bird squawks from the animal guests:

God of the sparrow
God of the whale
God of the swirling stars
How does the creature say Awe
How does the creature say Praise

The last time we were at St. Luke's, in 2019, we had brought pictures of Rudi's Westies, Josh and Jake, and I had carried a little photo of my cat Liebchen, all blessed by Rev. Daniel Fournier along with Freddie, in the beautiful historical chapel.

This time, because of COVID-19, we were seated outside on the grass. Father Fournier remembered Freddie. As we put Freddie in front of him, I told Father Fournier about his cancer and that he was doing well under chemotherapy thus far. He laid a hand on Freddie's head and gave him a special blessing, and later came over to talk to us. "Love will protect him," he said.

Rudi and I had just been talking about Albus Dumbledore, the great wizard from the Harry Potter series, and his statement about love—that having been greatly loved greatly protects.

I think, in some respects, Freddie's love is protecting us all.

OCTOBER 16

Bill's birthday. This is Freddie's fourth chemotherapy treatment, and he will be first seen by a cardiologist to determine the health of his heart. He will be in the hospital most of the day.

I am always afraid this is too much for him, and then he comes bounding out, full of joy to see us. I hope all will be well. And surely it must be, because to distract myself I was checking out new posts on a Facebook page about old church monuments just now and up came a stained-glass window depicting St. Roch and his faithful canine companion, from the legend in which the saint, who was ill, was nursed back to health by a dog.

Later, Dr. Herrera called. "There is no recurrence of the cancer," she said, with a tone of pleasant surprise.

We spoke by phone, but I could hear her smile.

NOVEMBER 2

Gave Freddie his weekly medicated bath and noticed how thin his hair is getting. Is this a chemo side effect? It is sad that we have fought so hard to keep his coat through his bouts of alopecia and it was doing so well. But I'd rather have him bald, happy, and alive than a furry fuzzball of limited life.

Now that we have the BCSPCA 2021 Calendars, with Freddie as Man of March, I mailed out several more to those who voted for him, using his paw stamp to sign them.

Back in July, did we ever think we'd still have him in our lives?

NOVEMBER 13

A lucky day for Freddie—after his fifth and final chemotherapy induction, he was presented with a certificate of graduation, signed by Dr. Herrera and all the staff. It reads:

> This is to certify that Freddie has successfully completed his prescribed course of chemotherapy with utmost bravery and distinction this 13th day of November 2020. Congratulations from the entire staff of BBVHS, we wish you all the best!

Among the lovely comments written on the certificate, Dr. Herrera's keeps us smiling: "Congrats, you handsome fella! You did it!"

NOVEMBER 15

We took a copy of the 2021 BCSPCA calendar to give to Dr. Mulley and staff, and to show them the graduation certificate. The entire place applauded. "He's the little dog that could, and can," said one of the vet techs.

Buoyed by what is to all intents and purposes remission from hemangiosarcoma, which we are told is very unusual and so might not be true, though if it is, it's only a bit short of miraculous, we have decided to list our condo and leave Victoria for the safety and, for Freddie, the familiarity of Sidney.

However much time he has left, we want it to be the best time possible.

CHAPTER EIGHT

The Cure for Anything

MOVING AWAY FROM VICTORIA to a new life elsewhere was not as easy as we would have preferred, in the full flush of euphoria after Freddie's successful completion of his chemotherapy course.

I did not make things better when, one night just before Christmas, I became very dizzy, then very sick, and after being taken to hospital was found to have put on a replay of a bleeding ulcer that had nearly killed me in 2005.

Back then, I had also been living through another period of unrelenting stress and worry, and clearly the stomach problems I had been having since summer were not just nervous indigestion. I spent several days in hospital hooked up to tubes, tapping out instructions on my cell phone to Rudi, just before being put under for an endoscopy, regarding Freddie's medications and feeding schedule.

After I was discharged and went home, Freddie stayed beside me on our bed, never leaving me except to eat, drink, or be taken outside. I took a photo of the two of us casualties, flat out, pressing against each other on the duvet, healing together.

I soon was almost back to my former self, and the stressors now were good ones. Waiting downstairs in the building's recreation room with Freddie as prospective buyers toured our home was a pleasure; packing china and our thousands of books and organizing storage and figuring out how to protect Freddie from the chaos of the actual move (he and Rudi stayed in a hotel in Sidney while I supervised the job)—all of it gave me joy.

Best of all, we had engineered a coup on a footing with Freddie's miraculous remission. My ex-husband Les was planning to retire and move up island, meaning he would be selling his condo in Sidney near Amherst Beach, in the new year. The province and, indeed, the nation were still in the grip of a real estate boom, perhaps as much because of COVID-19 as despite it, and many available properties that we'd toured and liked and were dog-friendly and ticked most of the boxes were sold almost overnight.

When Les discovered our plans, he asked if we'd like to buy his place. The pluses were many. Freddie already knew it, having stayed there with him when Rudi and I were in the UK for my *Lost War Horses of Cairo* book tour in 2018. The neighborhood was located just north of Sidney, in the vicinity of the miniature perfection of Amherst Beach, which Freddie loved to visit. The unit had a small, secluded garden with patio, where Freddie could spend time outside. Sidney was a quiet, safe community where everyone already knew Freddie and us. And we even got to take a "test drive," staying over on New Year's Eve. We took possession of the property in February 2021, Freddie and Rudi keeping to the bedroom—which we set up in advance—while I got the rest of the house organized.

Now that we lived beside the ocean again, I had reason to recall a famous line in the short story, *The Deluge at Norderney*, written by Danish writer Isak Dinesen in 1934, about how the cure for anything could be found in salt water: sweat, tears, or the sea. We could now say we had tried all three.

BESIDES STARTING A NEW and, we hoped, more pleasant life for Freddie, I had opportunity to dive back into work on *Muggins*, which was now due to appear in October from Heritage House in Victoria.

I began to collect illustrations and purchase rights to use them and other materials; I interviewed members of a family in Australia whose grandfather, an Anglo-Canadian soldier who'd been a POW in Germany throughout World War I, claimed he'd have starved to death but for the food packets sent to him from Canada via the funds Muggins raised collecting coins in Victoria; I visited archives, which were starting to open up again, slowly, and doubled down on research. Throughout the process, Freddie was always nearby, on the sofa or rug, as I worked at my desk, or at my feet as I sat on our patio, weather permitting, with my notebook.

The news on Freddie's hemangiosarcoma continued to be good. We took him to see Dr. Herrera at Boundary Bay every three months, with visits to Stanley Park. Some years earlier, while we still lived in Vancouver, we had purchased a stroller specially made for small dogs, which we thought at the time to use when we took Freddie to farmer's markets or other crowded situations that scared him. When he first became ill, I thought we might soon be using it to take him everywhere, but his strength, which his vets noticed, continued, even if his hair was coming back slowly and in peculiar patches. All that mattered was that he was still here, and that he was happy to be here.

One memory from that spring lingers because it demonstrates, despite his body's increasing weakness, just how strong Freddie's spirit remained. Even though we made him as comfortable as we could, Freddie did not like it when we went out on brief errands and left him at home. He was confined to a bedroom, where he had a fourposter bed all to himself, a water dish, two toy boxes, and a white noise machine we'd bought for our Victoria condo to dim the chaos from our neighbor— Freddie seemed to like the sound effects of "lakeside campfire." The air conditioning came on as required, but you'd think we'd consigned him to Alcatraz. He became especially upset when Rudi had to leave, despite my being home. As Rudi sneaked out, I would distract Freddie with a treat (though he soon figured out what I was up to, as all dogs do eventually) or a toy, or just stroke him, but it was always the same: running to the door or window and barking and whining his displeasure, then coming to me for solace.

That spring, Rudi finally received his notice to appear for his COVID-19 vaccination, which was offered at the Mary Winspear Centre in downtown Sidney. Freddie, resting on the bed, warily watched him dress. When it came time to go, Rudi went out the glass door into the garden while I held the struggling dog. It was like trying to wrestle a bear who was considerably slowed down by heart medication.

I put him on the floor and he ran to the garden door. For more than an hour, the dog who was finding it increasingly difficult to walk his usual distance, who was now more comfortable lying down than being on his feet, stood riveted at the door. I couldn't tempt him away with even his favorite fish treat. So I sat there quietly taking in what I was seeing.

The green garden outside, birds fluttering at the feeder, daffodils waving in the sea breeze. Our old Turkish kilim rug, glowing pink and blue in the light. And the silhouette against the brilliant foliage of a little dog, almost hairless still from chemotherapy, his tail transformed from a fluffy feather duster to a curling bald pigtail, standing still, alert, waiting. Loving.

On Rudi's return, far from being tired out from the effort of the wait, Freddie jumped with joy.

BY MARCH 2021, *MUGGINS* was in production, Freddie was in good form, and I began to think yet again of the book about Flush.

My enthusiasm for life in general was greater than it had been in years, fueled by relief at Freddie's health and our move to a community we loved. The astonished oncologist had told us that Freddie's being alive almost a year after a diagnosis of an aggressive cancer was well nigh a miracle, by some lucky alignment of the stars. It felt as if a door had opened.

Part of what intrigued me about Flush was not just his similarities to Freddie—both born in obscure settings then raised to prominence by adoption into a completely foreign but enriching environment—but of what had happened to teenaged me. Born in a village in the Sierra Nevada foothills, I was different from other boys, from the cradle onward, easy prey to bullying from my first day of school. Years of this led to a nervous breakdown in my second year of high school and suicidal ideation, followed by mandatory sessions with a psychologist. My parents, who had tried everything and knew their limitations, sought the advice of friends of theirs, William Luce and Ray Lewis. Bill, a renowned playwright (his one-woman play on Emily Dickinson, *The Belle of Amherst,* made Broadway history in 1976 when it won actress Julie Harris her fifth Tony Award), and Ray, a successful furniture designer and artist, had been together for over thirty years. They lived on ten acres outside Yosemite National Park, my old family setting for life transformations, in a glass and cedar chalet. Next door lived Bill's mother, and his sister was just down the road. When they heard what I was experiencing, Bill and Ray offered to take me for the summer, to have a chance of peace, quiet, reading, writing, music study, and supportive circumstances. For lack of a more precise term describing our relationship, I refer to Bill and Ray as my godfathers. A godparent pledges to help with the upbringing of a child, and though I was beyond childhood, this is what Bill, Ray, and their family did for me. The family completely embraced me, and that summer turned into a friendship of over forty years. Through them, through travel, exposure to gifted people in the arts, and freedom to grow into who I was meant to be, I became a writer. And I became me.

So I knew something of what I was doing when I guided Freddie, as I had been carefully guided, through the unknown and sometimes scary new experiences of life, as Flush also was guided by Elizabeth Barrett

Browning through London, Paris, and Florence. I felt ready to take on what I believed would be my best biography of a dog, a cross between the nonfiction and the magical realism I'd used in my biography of Woo. I would use the same techniques to treat the life of a dog who, after his death in June 1854, was immortalized first in paper and ink in the published letters of Elizabeth Barrett Browning and Robert Browning and all the biographies of them that followed their deaths. Then he was brought to life on stage by Besier in the 1930 play *The Barretts of Wimpole Street*, which in turn inspired Woolf to write her 1933 novelized biography, *Flush: A Biography*. Flush had lived almost as long as Woolf's Orlando, while never changing form.

Directly upon being born at the Hogarth Press in 1933, *Flush: A Biography* garnered every shade of faint praise, and some outright criticism. For one thing, even dog lovers had a hard time taking Flush Barrett Browning seriously. In his *Book of Famous Dogs*, Albert Payson Terhune disapproved of both the real Flush and a dog actor he once saw playing Barrett Browning's dog in a performance of Besier's play; he said the real Flush was a distraction in Barrett Browning's life of creativity and purpose, and he criticized the dog actor for upstaging the human drama in the play.

As a biographer of animals, I have special reason to appreciate the literary sleight of hand, and the pondering of complex animal psychology, involved in the task of writing in the genre. It is, as I once wrote, somewhat like the writing of a saint's life. That charismatic persona was once a real person but left no written records, only acts of kindness that laid brief but unforgettable shadows across the lives of ordinary people. These impressions passed from lips to ear until codified in literary form in a story about an unknowable being, layered with repeated lacquerings of love. The result is an account of a life we know is unreliable but still feel is true, much as we presume to know the affections of a dog who can prove it to us in ways not always easy to understand.

I was curious about Woolf's motivation for and methods in writing about Flush. After watching that single performance of *The Barretts of Wimpole Street* at the Queen's Theatre, the canine star of which was a cocker spaniel called Tuppenny of Ware, Woolf returned to the writings of Elizabeth and Robert, from which the idea for a "life" formed. The idea seized her to the point where she had to begin immediately. I took a deep dive into the same writings and found much rich detail that her novel does not include.

To begin with, there was the fascinating Mary Russell Mitford, sitting in her Three Mile Cross cottage in Berkshire, in her odd clothes and surrounded by her beloved dogs, writing novels and stories and plays to keep a less friendly canine (the wolfish debt collector) from the door. In her plumpness, gentility, and keen sense of humour, she served as a sort of fairy godmother to village lads in need of someone to listen to and care for them, as well as to employ them. Her correspondence, letter after glowing letter, to Elizabeth Barrett, who lived in a dark room at the back of 50 Wimpole Street, London, reads today like social media texts of an especially learned quality, shared by women from opposite ends of the earth.

It was Mitford who, on hearing of the tragic death by drowning of Elizabeth Barrett's brother at Torquay, Devonshire, in 1840, suggested that one of the puppies fathered by her spaniel, Flush—formerly the dog of Ben Embery, Mitford's young servant—might be a companion to Elizabeth in her loss. Mitford was eccentric but wise in the ways of world and heart. She believed that Flush the Second would prove revitalizing for Elizabeth, and she was right, beyond expectations. A silky brown cocker spaniel, Flush became Elizabeth's *compagnon de voyage* in her landlocked back bedroom, sleeping on her bed, sharing her meals, resting his chin on the end of her manuscripts as the verses and translations flowed from her pen. Her pain for the loss of her brother ebbed, and her writing, her one solid handgrip in a life over which she had no control, filled the emptiness again.

But life at 50 Wimpole Street was deceptively quiet, as it was in Mitford's cottage in tiny Three Mile Cross. Both were settings for hidden dramas and close-kept secrets that were to explode the invisible prison walls of accepted manners and mores of "good society." In Mitford's case, her dignified and dutiful lady's maid, Kerenhappuch Taylor, known as "K.," a young Yorkshire woman named for a daughter of Job, became pregnant not once but twice by Ben Embery, whom Mitford loved like a son. It was his Flush who fathered Elizabeth Barrett's Flush. Until the scandal drove him out of Three Mile Cross to an early and obscure death in Brixton, Lambeth (across the river from the Barretts' neighborhood but another universe away in accessibility), Ben regularly asked Elizabeth, through Mitford's letters, if Flush was happy in his new home.

Flush witnessed a scandal on his own turf, amid the more well-appointed rooms of the Barrett household. His mistress accepted the marriage proposal of Robert Browning, and in September 1846, with Flush under one arm, Elizabeth fled Wimpole Street and her father, sailing for Italy with Browning. In Florence, where they settled, the little dog who had been born in rural Berkshire was petted by princes and poets, mesmerists and monks; climbed volcanoes and slept on palace floors; and apparently added to the canine population of the city when he wasn't feasting on bunches of grapes pulled fresh off the vine, according to Barrett Browning. (Grapes are toxic to dogs, so either the poet was exaggerating or Flush was super-canine.)

Flush was part of Barrett Browning's life for thirteen years. After the birth of her son, Pen, Flush was no longer the center of her life, and he gradually faded away. In June 1854, he died at the age of fourteen—wheezing, overweight, and bald from alopecia—and was buried under the cellar floor of the Brownings' home, Casa Guidi.

And there he would stay, until Flush as memory and inspiration would re-emerge that night in 1930 when Woolf, observing the antics of Tuppenny of Ware in *The Barretts of Wimpole Street*, returned home with the seed of a book that was to be her bestselling volume to date. Woolf considered *Flush* a "joke," a playful jab at her friend Lytton Strachey's *Lives of Eminent Victorians*. Yet in the story, Woolf seems to be responding to Barrett Browning's credulity in matters spiritualistic. She conjures the ghostly flicker of a fluffy tail, the shine of bright eyes, and through those eyes paints the world of the English countryside and beyond. From London to Florence, Flush walks with his mistress at the side of the literary greats of the nineteenth century, with all their human failings and foibles. Woolf sketches a view of unexamined lives through the least examined of lives: the animal companion, with whom many of us experience everything that makes life worth living, but to whom we assign, too often, not even a supporting actor role, but a mere walk-on appearance.

Perhaps I could do the same—jump from the living dog, who dies and is buried, who then leaps from his grave in Florence to the stages of Broadway and the West End and the studios of Hollywood, onto the pages of a famous novelist who knew all about ghosts and the strange passage of time. I once put down my edition of the collected poems of Elizabeth Barrett Browning, a volume from the 1900s I'd inherited from a Scottish great-grandaunt, open to the page where the poem "To Flush, My Dog" was printed, and when I came back into the room, Freddie was licking the page in his mysterious, charming way. It felt like a blessing.

BUT IT WASN'T TO be. Something else was not right with Freddie, but it was at least something about which we were already aware. After several weeks of more or less normal life in his new home, his heart cough had returned. Unless you have heard a heart cough, you may not know what it is—even hearing it for the first time, it's hard to know what to make of it.

Freddie had long been prey to a Pomeranian genetic inheritance, the reverse sneeze. I first saw it happen in our kitchen a year after we'd adopted him. At first, watching him inhale, wheeze, snort, stand with legs splayed out and eyes staring forward, I thought Freddie was having a life-threatening seizure. But it is for the most part not a dangerous thing. It is caused by the long snout of the dog's physiognomy, prompted by an allergic reaction or stress or water taken in the wrong way. The dog is not suffocating or seizuring; what is happening is a forceful, sudden, abnormal inhalation through the nose. This causes a honking snort, similar in sound to when a person clears phlegm from their throat, but in a repeated paroxysm, as if the dog cannot take in enough air. Reverse sneezing can sometimes be a symptom of a serious underlying condition, such as a collapsed trachea or a problem in the sinuses. We had Freddie checked out the first few times and everything was fine. The way we handled it was to stroke his chest and head and tell him it would soon be over. Once it stopped, he would usually be up for playing or drinking some water.

Heart cough is another matter. In a dog diagnosed, as Freddie had been, with mitral valve disease, the cough is a function of pulmonary edema caused by a heart unable to do its work efficiently, allowing a buildup of fluid in the lungs. We had been told by Dr. Mulley in Victoria that Freddie's heart murmur was at stage 3 or even stage 4, hence the medication to help him function normally. All medications require periodic adjusting for one reason or another; human patients with cardiac issues know all about this. What the condition also means is that the patient is not receiving enough oxygen, which can lead to dizziness, nausea, and so on.

Because our attention was primarily on Freddie's remission status, we only realized gradually that something wasn't right with his pulmonary health. But through the spring and early summer of 2021, concerns about his breathing brought us to his new veterinarian, Dr. Brad McKell at Sidney Animal Hospital, the clinic we'd taken Freddie to prior to my move to Vancouver and the one where we said goodbye to Jessie in 2008.

Dr. McKell's examination indicated that Freddie's heart murmur had progressed to stage 5, the most serious. He explained that there was still no reason, beyond the care we were already giving him (not walking him more than just the front lawn in hot weather, letting him tell us how far was far enough), to be overly worried. A dog, even in its teens as Freddie was, can live for years with an advanced heart murmur, especially when administered medications to manage it.

On top of the other medications we were giving Freddie, Dr. McKell prescribed a diuretic to help rid his body of excess fluid, taking pressure off his lungs and easing his breathing issues. This proved to be successful, but it also increased his thirst, and made him prone to wetting in the house before we could get him outside. So for the first time, we put diapers on him at night, and he took to the change better than we expected.

By this time, I had drawn up a medications schedule that was taped to a door of the kitchen cabinet in which we kept all of Freddie's canned and dry food, treats, and supplements—a full three shelves. When you are caring for a dog prescribed with several medications, some that can't be taken too close to one another, some to be taken with food and some without, you can't dispense it whenever you think about it—at least, I could not. I had to see what he needed at a particular time of day, and this became more important as the medications increased.

I had had some practice in this. Ever since my cancerous thyroid was removed in 1997, I take a daily thyroid hormone replacement tablet, but ingesting it is not as easy as it sounds. You cannot eat or drink anything for an hour afterward, meaning that if you have an early morning job to get ready for, you must get up extra early to take the pill, then shower and shave and get ready, then gulp down your breakfast after the appointed sixty minutes and rush out the door. This schedule aligns with having a dog eager to go out first thing, so timing medication doses was never a problem for me, and I could imagine that as Freddie aged and the medications changed or became more complicated, I'd be able to figure out how to make it all work so that he got what he needed.

The issue was getting the pills into Freddie. Many animal guardians know what a battle of wills this can lead to, with depressing regularity, made the worse by the fact that while you are cramming meds down your dog's throat for his own good, you feel terrible for having to do it and guilty that you have not found a better way. Luckily, though Freddie wouldn't let me pick him up off his territory—our bed, the sofa—he was fine with me parting his jaws to get the medicine to go down, all thanks to our helpful friend Monica at Reigning Cats and Dogs. The secret was liverwurst. "You can get them to take anything if it has liverwurst on it," she told me. So where, eleven years earlier, while building trust with Freddie by hand feeding him, I had canned dog food fingers, now I had fingers permanently redolent of liverwurst. It became a sort of perfume that I began to enjoy, because it was the secret to keeping Freddie well, and keeping Freddie well made the pronounced effort so worth it. As Barrett Browning wrote of Flush,

> *Little canst thou joy or do,*
> *Thou who lovest greatly.*[1]

Freddie made the act of loving him so easy, not just because he was adorable but because, when he saw we were distressed, despite his own problems, he never hesitated to comfort us, the way Flush did for his mistress. As they were with Flush, these sweet traits were part of his nature.

CHAPTER NINE

His Good Deeds Linger

WE CONSIDERED OURSELVES LUCKY—and we were, more than we fully understood. It's the way of good fortune to make us thankful and at the same time unaware of just how fortunate we are.

During the heat dome of summer 2021, we ensured Freddie suffered no distress, a heart condition and heat being two things that did not do well together. We mostly stayed in the bedroom with the air conditioning unit, purchased a year earlier to keep Freddie cool in our too-warm Victoria condo.

He was noticeably slowing down. We tried to be prepared for it, but we could not be prepared for how abruptly his heart condition would make changes we had assumed would be gradual. On an afternoon of blessedly normal temperatures, helped by sea breezes, we took Freddie on his now usual route around our small block. He had once enjoyed walking down to Roberts Bay and around Sidney when we went shopping along Beacon Avenue, but his tiredness prompted us to shorten these jaunts until, now, the block was his limit.

This particular day, we were within sight of our garden and almost home when Freddie stood still, then tottered. Rudi caught him and carried him into the coolness of the house. After he'd sat a few minutes on the bed, he was more his normal self, but life had changed again. We stopped going more than half a block, sometimes a little farther, and that seemed to suit Freddie just fine.

Looking back through my diary, I see how increasingly Freddie was becoming an invalid, held back physically by his failing heart and the breathing difficulties this caused. But he was never morose, never complained, not unlike my late father, whose emphysema kept him attached to oxygen 24/7 at the end but did nothing to daunt his good cheer. He'd call us up, taking gulps of air every few words, to say, "I don't care how you guys are, how's my favorite mutt?"

Animals are like mirrors. Their uncomplicated, easily satisfied, ever hopeful natures show us what we lack in those areas as humankind, giving us the opportunity to emulate them, to bring our better angels to the fore. Sometimes when we three were in the bedroom for our nightly TV hour, I'd sense Freddie looking at me. I would look over at him, and seeing him gazing my way with shining chocolate pudding eyes, my fears for his health were instantly calmed, bringing me back to the moment—no past regret, no future angst, just the pure and wonderful now.

BY AUGUST, THE WORST of the heat had settled into a more normal level. When earlier in the summer it felt as if we were up to our noses in a hot bath, now it was down around our ankles. We were happy all over again that we'd moved to Sidney, where the sea from three directions funneled cool and salty air into our leafy garden, where Freddie enjoyed relaxing on an old Chinese carpet whose softened surfaces had provided comfort for many past animal companions in my family.

In July, despite Freddie's occasional breathing issues, he had passed a five-hour session with his oncologist in Langley, who declared him still in remission from hemangiosarcoma, marking a remarkable year for him. It was heartening to see professionals smile and exclaim what a fighter Freddie was and that they had not heard of another dog living so long after so dire a diagnosis. We sailed on that cloud for a while.

A strange and upsetting event occurred to unsettle the still pool of our lives. We had a bird feeder outside the bedroom window. Freddie enjoyed watching the fluttering from his station on the bed, and we enjoyed watching him as his head turned to follow the darting bodies of various sizes and species, all jockeying for position.

One particular evening, when it was still light and warm and we were preparing to watch TV with Freddie, I noticed him standing on the bed and staring fixedly out the window at some avian commotion. Thinking there was a fight going on, I approached the window to tap on it and break it up when I saw what Freddie had seen: a female sparrow had somehow got her leg caught in a crimped area of the fence we'd placed around that part of the garden so the local cats wouldn't kill our birds. When I examined the bird close up, I saw the leg could not be saved, and from thrashing around the bird had damaged herself.

This was a Sunday, so no wildlife rescue center was open, and even our local vet was closed. That left the

Central Victoria Veterinary Hospital, where we'd taken
Freddie for some diagnostics during his chemotherapy
course last year. I managed to get the poor bird out of the
fencing (which we later removed) and into a box, then
dashed down the highway to the hospital. I knew there
was no way it could be saved and that I had been given
the role of angel of death, but I remembered something
written by Dorothy Brooke, subject of my 2018 book *The
Lost War Horses of Cairo*. As she looked over the week's
work horses, brought in by poor men grateful for a few
dollars to be relieved of a sick animal, deciding which
ones were to be euthanized and which could hold up
for rehabilitation, Mrs. Brooke would find her heart
entangled with a particular horse. This animal had
known kind care once but had been brutalized through
hard labor and the absence of any veterinary attention
for a variety of ailments. It responded to her English
words and voice, as if remembering its English origin.
She wished she could hang on to such spirits as this,
she wrote, to make them better through some magical alchemy of wishful thinking and funding and extra
time she did not have, but she could only order the
horse humanely put down because there was simply no
other course to take. Its suffering, which had gone on
for years already, absolutely had to stop, and she had
to be the agent for making that happen, as grievous as
the duty was.

I love sparrows, though there are so many of them
and their song is sharp and shrill. I felt the weight of
responsibility for ending this one's suffering as quickly
as possible. I wondered whether she still had a nest
somewhere, with babies needing to be fed, and if that
was why she had struggled so much that she hurt herself

further. I wondered how her day had started, that bright blue morning and golden afternoon, only to end so sadly.

As I handed the box over to the veterinary technician who answered the door buzzer, I tried to explain what had happened. The young man cradled the box and touched my arm, saying that they would make sure she didn't suffer. I returned to my car and cried. When I got home, Freddie sat with me as I pulled out a book of verse about birds. I was moved to re-read "To a Sparrow," a poem by William Carlos Williams. High in the clouds, Williams writes, this drab gray creature soars to places we on earth can only imagine— underscoring the importance, the dignity, and the beauty of all lives, sparrows and saints together.[1] The words echoed the ache in my heart.

How often I thought of that day, that bird, in the months to come, when we were to see a lot more of Central Victoria Veterinary Hospital, this time for another fragile animal.

WHEN HIS COUGH RETURNED and even upping his medications didn't seem to help as it once had, we took Freddie in to see Dr. McKell. We also wanted to ask him about something we'd noticed while giving Freddie his weekly bath. Both Rudi and I felt swollen lymph nodes in Freddie's neck. Our first thought was that it was related to some infection. That was what Dr. McKell assumed too, when we first brought Freddie into the clinic in mid-August. He decided to perform an aspiration biopsy just in case.

A few days later, as I was walking through downtown Sidney, having just picked up some treats for Freddie and some canned food to tempt his uncertain appetite, my phone rang. It was Dr. McKell. He asked me if I was in a place where he could talk to me, so I moved off the sidewalk into a shaded area outside the pet supply business I had just visited. He told me tests indicated that Freddie had lymphoma.

I thought back to a little over a year ago, when we'd met Dr. Mulley from a safe distance in the parking lot of her clinic in Victoria and she said the C-word. And here I was, again, outside, under a cloudless blue sky, happy summering folks all around me, as my heart froze.

Dr. McKell asked if I wanted to do another round of chemotherapy. To be fair, he said, it had to be noted that Freddie's heart was not in good shape. Chemotherapy seemed to have worked fine for him the previous year, but he was not as strong now. Putting him on a palliative track was an option that we might want to consider.

In the next few moments of silence, which felt like a weirdly timeless interlude of racing thoughts, I sat down and looked at the sky from behind a potted crocosmia, the red blooms darting forward on bright green stems. I had a decision to make, with no time to confer with Rudi. How much time would Freddie have, anyway? He now had two cancers, and a heart that increasingly could not do its job. I asked myself, what is right for him? I also asked my beloved dead, who would have known what to say, what I should do. I asked each of them— parents, grandparents, aunts, friends, St. Francis: What would you have me do? And the one image that stood out was a video I still had on my phone from Easter. Freddie had had one of his good days, really good days. We'd thrown his rabbit toy, given to him a decade earlier by my late godfather, into the middle of the living room.

Though his hair was getting lighter with age, and most of it had fallen out from chemotherapy, and he was a little slower than before, Freddie dashed after his rabbit, running around the room, shaking the life out of it. He had shown some of that spirit only the previous day, while we were waiting for this call that had now come. I couldn't let him go while he still had such a love of life, while being with us gave him such pleasure, gave us such hope. I asked if Dr. McKell could give us another referral to Boundary Bay in Langley.

I got home, slipped in the garden door, and put my head around the bedroom doorway. Rudi and Freddie were on the bed. Rudi was reading, his hand on Freddie's back. Freddie looked up, having heard the crackling of the shopping bag and knowing it contained treats. I asked Rudi to come to the kitchen to see something special I'd got for Freddie. "Stay here," Rudi said to the pup who always obeyed him.

I told Rudi what I knew and that I had asked Dr. McKell to provide a referral for another course of chemotherapy. Then we stood in the kitchen, holding each other, sobbing into each other's shoulders as quietly as we could. By now, Freddie had jumped down off the bed to come and join us. On hearing his toenails clicking on the wooden hallway floor, Rudi and I pulled apart, putting on smiles we didn't feel. I said, opening a bag, "Look, sweetheart! See what I brought!"

When we reached her by phone later, Freddie's favorite oncologist and biggest fan, Dr. Herrera, just said, "Oh, no. No." But we pulled ourselves together and began to climb another mountain. We decided, in the interests of not wishing to lose precious time, to go with what is called CHOP treatment, a chemotherapy regimen whose

acronym is taken from the primary drugs used: cyclophos-
phamide, hydroxydaunorubicin, vincristine (Oncovin),
and prednisone. There was no time to waste. From the
date of diagnosis, without any treatment, the prognosis
for Freddie's lymphoma was no more than four to six
weeks of life. With treatment, Freddie could live one or
more years, maybe several years, as the remission rate
was very high.

My diary, which had been quiet and filled mostly with
daily observations of Freddie's breathing, his medication
adjustments, and hopeful comments based on good days
weighed against bad, now became what it was the year
before: a daily march toward an unknown destination.

– Freddie Diary 2021 –

AUGUST 22

After the euphoria of declaring battle, the morning brought
fears and morbid fantasies and self-recriminations. Had
we caught it too late? We talked at breakfast about what
to do, not speaking certain words, though Freddie would
not have known what we were saying, sitting there watching us and mostly interested in a treat from the table. I
agonized over putting him through procedures that will
wear him down further. He seems so fragile, yet then he
jumps up and is as keen as ever. Rudi says, "As long as he
wants to be with us, we should help him."

AUGUST 24

We sailed today to Salt Spring Island to see Freddie's
groomer from Vancouver, Elaine. I had told her about
the diagnosis. She handles him so tenderly, made him so
beautiful—the tragedy being that his fur had started to

come back in again, and now, with more chemotherapy, it will start falling out. She said, "What matters is that he is happy," and tied a little tartan bandana around his neck. She gave him a reiki treatment, too. If love can heal, he's better already.

AUGUST 26

Freddie's Gotcha Day. A far cry from any we've had for him before. We sailed over for his examination at Boundary Bay Veterinary Specialty Hospital. Stanley Park is too far away, and we cannot tire him by taking him there, so we went to Centennial Beach. It's a calming place—the soft silver of sand dunes and brittle silver of beach grass, the hard blue of the ocean and, above, the soft blue of the sky. I snapped a photo of Freddie and Rudi on a driftwood log, Freddie in his blue jacket looking with fascination at some water birds, as if seeing a sign and a wonder. They were indeed.

AUGUST 29

Freddie's coughing continues. His hydrocodone syrup seems to work but makes him drowsy. He no longer wants the cookies we got him for TV time, although he will eat meat treats, the smellier the better. We are grateful for that and for every smallest thing.

SEPTEMBER 4

Gave Freddie his cough suppressant pill at bedtime and had a quiet night, but today he coughed several times and was not interested in his walk. While on his cough meds, he has strong dreams, like he used to do when we first brought him home. *What are you running from? I wish we knew and could make you less afraid of it.*

SEPTEMBER 5

A complete change today. All seems relatively normal. Freddie had some bouts of coughing but was up for a walk around the block and later down to Roberts Bay. He loves the sand when the tide has washed out, leaving behind all sorts of smelly things. And he stands and stares at the herons, who stand and stare at him. Later, Les came down from the farm to visit, and it was sweet seeing them together. Freddie remembers his first alpha dad—shows him the deference to authority and the respect you might see a well-brought up child exhibit toward its elders. He still loves Les, but when he had finished saying hello, Freddie jumped up on the sofa beside Rudi and pressed against him, as if to reassure him.

SEPTEMBER 14

I spoke with Dr. McKell about switching Freddie's chemotherapy protocol to Central Veterinary Hospital in Victoria. It's nowhere near as far as it is to the mainland, and there would be far less stress getting him there. It is sad that Freddie won't see Dr. Herrera or the staff of Boundary Bay again under these circumstances, but his lymph nodes are shrinking and maybe, just maybe, they can meet again under happier conditions. He beat the worst cancer devil in the books. Why not this one?

SEPTEMBER 18

It is so much easier taking Freddie the comparably short distance to Victoria. So far, no bad side effects from the chemotherapy. Freddie did wet his diaper and some got on his blanket, which we have to wash carefully because of the chemo in his bloodstream and fluids. He ate dinner heartily. Pants a bit before bed but coughing minimal. He hasn't had his anti-tussive syrup in a week and I'm loathe to start it unless we absolutely have to as it makes him so drowsy and seems to prompt bad dreams.

SEPTEMBER 30

Dr. Orna Kristal, Freddie's oncologist, is like all his other specialists, merely a voice coming from my phone, thanks to social distancing protocols. But she has a warm, comforting timbre, like the teacher who reads to class in the afternoon, and she isn't afraid to talk about his heart, which to her is the primary concern. She is astounded that Freddie did so well with hemangiosarcoma, but his heart continues to concern her. She doesn't want to shorten his life on that score in trying to lengthen it with chemotherapy. Another problem: because doxorubicin (hydroxydaunorubicin) was used in the five treatments that seem to have knocked out his hemangiosarcoma, he can only have one more dose, and while it is effective, it is hard on the heart. She wants to save it as the silver bullet, the dose of last resort. He sits on Rudi's lap, listening to all this, looking at me, as I try to smile back at him.

OCTOBER 4, FEAST OF ST. FRANCIS

What a different day from past feasts of St. Francis. We considered taking Freddie to be blessed again at St. Luke's, but this time his chemotherapy has him down for the count and his appetite is affected. I went shopping for all sorts of tinned fish, tripe, steak. I am hand feeding him now. At least he eats when I do that. Dr. Kristal called to recommend an ACE inhibitor for his heart.

OCTOBER 5

Freddie wouldn't even eat chopped steak—though I managed to get his liver pill down him. I talked to Dr. McKell about prescribing an inappetence drug. Freddie had diarrhea and there were assorted issues all day. By the end of the day, both Rudi and I are exhausted. I went outside to look at the stars and ask the apparently deaf universe: Why this? Why him? Why?

OCTOBER 6

Freddie slept through the night, but his temperature this morning was low. I kept taking it at intervals, and finally it reached the point where I called the Central clinic in Victoria. They said to bring him in ASAP. We handed him over and later, as we sat in the car, Dr. Elise Boller called us. She said this is about his heart disease, not a reaction to the chemotherapy. Rudi and I had just been talking about how, if only Freddie were dealing with one cancer plus heart trouble, or two cancers and no heart trouble, this would be so much easier for him. That this little guy, now thirteen or fourteen years old, should have to fight so outsized an enemy tests my resolve not to fall into anger, not to rage against a world that unfairly doles out misery to those least deserving of it. I try to see his cancer as I did last year—as a part of him, as I saw it for myself when I was diagnosed in 1997. I went to a concert the night before my surgery, listening to Schubert and Beethoven, welcoming my cancer to partake of this world of beauty one last time, a part of me but, like Freddie's cancer over two decades later, knowing that it cannot stay. I try to love the cancer out of him, if I can. There is nothing I will not do, including make friends with this deadly enemy, to save his life.

OCTOBER 7

Freddie was still in intensive care till this afternoon. We talked to the doctor about adjusting his medications at home, adding others. He was okay enough to be released to us this evening, and we settled in for the night, keeping a watch on him. We are to increase his diuretic meds, which we also have to watch because it leaches potassium, and that is part of his problem—his electrolytes were very low. But it's mostly his heart. His mitral valve disease is allowing fluid to back up in his lungs, and his heart just can't deal with it. Our poor boy.

OCTOBER 8

We took Freddie out to the lawn. He has bad diarrhea, but he's eager to eat certain things—they have to be smelly and fishy. By afternoon, I decided we had to take him back to Vic Central. He was in respiratory distress and having trouble walking, his tail and ears down, and has a slight head tremor. He also has a fever. At the hospital, they told us that with all his issues, it's not impossible to treat him or at least provide comfort, but that time is running out. With that question left in the air—should we consider ending his suffering? "The next hours are crucial." Oh my God, is this it?

OCTOBER 11, THANKSGIVING

We picked Freddie up at Vic Central. He had to spend part of the time in an oxygen cage, and we know he had a tube in his nose because one of the vet techs, seeing how upset we were, sent us a photo of him sitting in his stainless-steel kennel, soft blankets under him. She meant well, and the image was a kind of relief for us, showing he really was still here. But his eyes were the same ones we'd seen eleven years earlier, in the photos taken of him right after his rescue. "What's going to happen to me now?" they seemed to ask. Again, it is clear to the doctors that this is not related to the chemotherapy, but we are now talking seriously about taking him off of it and putting him on a palliative course, where what happens happens, and when it does, he's at home with us, where he loves to be—the only reason he is still here, after the events of the last few days, is because it's clear he loves us and his home. His joy at seeing us and being on the bed again, on coming home this morning, is heartbreaking, heart-filling—a Thanksgiving unlike any other and more precious than any other I have known.

OCTOBER 18

Freddie's breathing is sometimes labored, but he is eager to go outside, coughing a little, but enjoying his food. His belly is more distended, which is connected to his heart failure. It is both cute and terrible. Honoring professional commitments gave me some respite from what was hanging over us three. I gave an interview to CHEK News about *Muggins*, to be published in two days; I was on auto-pilot, but got through.

Then followed a Zoom talk of my book, hosted by bestselling dog author and fellow cancer survivor Teresa J. Rhyne.[2]

During the hour or so I was on screen, I lifted Freddie to my webcam so everyone taking part could see him. He was groggy, and his breathing concerned me. When I put him back on the floor, he tottered. As I continued to mindlessly chatter about Muggins, I held Freddie till he steadied himself against my leg and then listened as he slowly walked back to the bedroom and Rudi. There is something to the concept of telepathic love, because I was feeling it tonight, through the screen, from the hearts of people I don't even know.

It was for Freddie.

OCTOBER 19

Freddie's next chemotherapy treatment. He trotted with us right up to the door of Vic Central. We decided that because he seems to be stronger, it is the right thing to do, but only after a long pros and cons talk with Dr. Kristal. We hope and pray it is.

OCTOBER 20

Today, the box of my author's copies of *Muggins* arrived. Freddie has always loved helping me open boxes of author's copies, going back several books. This morning he sat while I undid the box, and then, when I pulled out a copy, he licked it in his mysterious and charming way. I shot some video of him doing this but didn't post to Facebook as he doesn't look himself, and indeed this was a private moment. I had a Zoom launch for *Muggins* tonight through Tanner's Books in Sidney, and while it would have been lovely to bring Freddie up to the screen for folks to see the dog who inspires me, as I had done for Teresa's program, he was just not himself and it would not have been fair to him.

I'm so happy everyone loves Muggins's story. So many seem moved that I am donating royalties to the BCSPCA and the Canadian Red Cross BC-Yukon. "It's all because of Freddie," I tell them. As if he knows, he didn't cough once till the show was over.

OCTOBER 21

Freddie ate decently today, but has been coughing and his appetite, though not nonexistent, still isn't what it was. It was a struggle getting his pills down him. I gave him an inappetence tablet to stimulate some interest in food. When the difficulties arise, I feel it is my fault they are happening, that I should be able to help him more, that I am not helping him. And I feel a strange change coming on, like the night a month ago when he stopped being interested in his favorite cookies at TV time. Some things change, though it is unimaginable that they should, and we watch the old ways wash down the sluice of time, unable to reverse the process, helpless.

OCTOBER 23

We bathed Freddie this morning, as he had had bad diarrhea. I was reminded, running warm soapy water over his body, of the night three years before, at our home in Victoria, when I sat in our bathroom terrified of the tarry diarrhea coming out of me—my own blood, coagulated; of my swimming head and racing heart; of having to kneel in the shower, because I couldn't stand, to wash myself clean preparatory to heading for Royal Jubilee emergency. I had knelt on a towel to dry myself off, and there at the open bathroom door stood Freddie. He was gazing at me with eyes full of fear but also that shining compassion I had seen at other times, other years, when he'd found me despairing over what had become of my life, consumed with fears of what would happen to him if I couldn't get myself back on my feet. It was a look I held in my mind as I lay dazed in hospital for the next forty-eight hours. I tried to give him that same wordless reassurance as we stood him on a towel, dried him off, told him how handsome he was.

FREDDIE

Today, Freddie allowed me to give him his usual medications without incident. There is some light at the end of the tunnel, I think, where his appetite is concerned, as he seems more into his treats than meals. A friend who has seen more than one dog through chemotherapy and knows how hard it is when they won't eat gave us a meatloaf recipe that has worked wonders: it's all Freddie wants to eat now, though I have to lace it with the smelly tripe that he needs to get his appetite going. I wonder why I was so despairing last night and am resolved to be more hopeful. Fingers crossed. I pray every night now. At least it makes me feel better.

OCTOBER 24

A good day! So much so, I left the house for an hour to sign copies of *Muggins* at Tanner's Books in Sidney, adding Freddie's pawtograph stamp to each. Came back bearing treats from Bosley's in crinkly bags and Freddie trotted alongside me to the kitchen, eager to see what I'd found for him. Is his appetite coming back? We hope so.

Such beautiful certainty of love, such trust in goodness.

I think he may be turning a corner in all this—I think we've pulled him back from the brink.

Maybe my prayers all this year are having an effect. *Maybe*.

ON OCTOBER 26, A day the calendar tells me was a Tuesday, I wrote an essay for the *Literary Review of Canada*.

The editor had contacted me, asking for a think piece on any topic, and when I asked if I might write about my dog, I had to tell him why and about what had happened the day before—that Freddie had died in Rudi's and my embrace in the ICU of Central Victoria Veterinary Hospital, after a pre-dawn race in the car from Sidney when it became clear he was unable to breathe. There was nothing more that could be done, staff told us, except to ease his suffering. As we approached and he was brought out of the oxygen cage to see us for the last time, our little dog stood up for us, wagging his tail, though barely able to breathe.

The editor was mortified, feeling, as anyone would, that he had blundered into my private despair. But this serendipitous test of my discipline was a heaven-sent opportunity, for the thousands of subscribers to the *Review* across Canada and around the world, for me to acknowledge, even while the pain was still so keen, how greatly Freddie had changed my life as writer and as man. It was a chance for me to share him, extending if not his physical life, then the memory of him, as I had tried to share his living presence in my books.

In those hard and empty days following Freddie's death, I thought a lot of lines written by English poet Mary Webb: "For there with shining eyes his good deeds linger."[3]

His did. His do.

My Brave Companion

S HORTLY AFTER DAWN ON October 25, 2021—606 years
to the day after the Battle of Agincourt—an embat-
tled warrior, about age thirteen, went to sleep in my
arms. My dog Freddie was no conventional soldier, but
he knew how to fight. He'd spent more than a year fend-
ing off a combination of heart disease and cancer, until
his frail body could fight no more.

Rescued from a dreadful trifecta of puppy mill
operator, backyard breeder, and hoarder, in the British
Columbia interior, Freddie came into my life in 2010,
when my partner and I met him at the BCSPCA branch
in Victoria. He was at least two years old, and he was
terrified of everything.

Puppy mills are work camps for dogs, places where
females are perpetually impregnated in substandard
settings, their pups taken away to serve as breeders
themselves or sold on. These are often animals of
pedigree—spitzes like Freddie, King Charles spaniels,
French bulldogs. Their progeny, rife with hidden genetic
flaws and saddled with neuroses, fetch high prices when
in the hands of unscrupulous proprietors—and when
would-be owners ask no questions.

Coming from such a place, Freddie had many fears.
We spent most of his eleven years with us helping him

dismantle them. While we never convinced him not to be terrified of other dogs, we did teach him how to play with toys. He also learned that the food and water we put out were all for him alone. Most amazingly, despite sufficient proof from the moment of his birth that our species is not always particularly lovable, he learned to trust and even to love humans.

As a biographer, and as the great-grandson of a suffragette, I've specialized in the lives of extraordinary but unsung women, those who made their mark in a man's world on their own terms. But when Freddie appeared on the scene, I began to think of the unexamined lives of animals, especially those we've conscripted into human wars.

The history of human-animal relationships is inspiring, but it is also terrible. Accounts of animals used in conflict are particularly so. It is rare to find written accounts of animals from before the Victorian era that are focused through a lens of compassion. Ironically, this is not the case for animals conscripted in the First World War. By then, generations of men had been brought up with dogs, had been raised to see animals as feeling beings worthy of kindness.

Through those soldiers' eyes, we meet such message-carrying pigeons as Cher Ami. Despite being shot in the breast, blinded, and blasted out of the sky by enemy fire only to rise again with a leg hanging by a tendon, Cher Ami flew a message through hell and saved an encircled battalion. In that same battle, the Meuse-Argonne offensive, a former Paris stray called Rags, adopted by the American First Division, shielded a battalion from destruction by running a message to artillery despite being wounded and gassed on the way.

I was raised by parents who took animals seriously and considered them part of the family. But it wasn't until I saw, through Freddie, what an animal risks to navigate a world of human use and abuse, and to not lose hope but forge ahead, that I understood my opportunity and my duty to give voice to the voiceless.

Freddie never stepped onto a battlefield, but his example led me to write about Rags; about the English general's wife, Dorothy Brooke, who saved thousands of former war horses abandoned in Egypt to lives of hard labor; about Woo, the magical and tragic monkey who inspired the artist Emily Carr; and, most recently, about Muggins, the fundraising spitz of Victoria, who in his short life collected thousands of dollars for the Red Cross, POWs, orphaned children, and injured animals of the Great War—animals who made a difference in human lives and human history.

The poet Mary Oliver wrote of her dog, Percy, "For he was made small but brave of heart." So are all our animal family: small, but brave. It's incumbent on us, I believe, to take their bravery seriously as they, in turn, unfailingly try to teach us the priceless lesson, despite all the risks and dangers, of saying yes to life, again and again and again.[1]

"A DOG REPRESENTS GRIEF built-in," writes Simon Garfield; "we acquire our friends with the knowledge that we will one day come to mourn them." But, as those who have been through this understand, we can never, ever know, even up to the last moments, how viscerally deep the anguish of that loss can be, or how long it lasts, and what indelible changes grief can work on the lives of survivors.[2]

His Good Deeds Linger

For myself, a year after Freddie's passing, while I am now able to write and talk about him without the stabs of anguish of earlier in the year, I look in the mirror each day to see a man with suddenly white hair, a face aged beyond recognition, with physical ailments not present before the hard year of 2020–21. A man who still has the occasional bad day, unable to believe Freddie is not waiting for me behind the door when I come home. Yes, we knew the day would come when, barring predeceasing him, we would send Freddie on another journey on which we could not follow. That day we could accept. It's the days after—the many, many days after—that proved challenging.

Thankfully, other people—many more than we realized—understand this grief, have experienced it, and reached out to comfort us. I placed Freddie's obituary in our local newspaper so that all the merchants up and down the high street, whom he had loved for their generous sharing of biscuits and kind greetings, would know of his death. I then posted words I almost couldn't believe I was writing on Facebook and in the groups I belonged to of pet parents with dogs dealing with cancer. Responses almost immediately came in. Emails, instant messages, letters, notes, cards, and flowers, as well as donations to animal charities in Freddie's name, began to arrive from what felt like the whole world at once.

And gifts, too. A friend in the US commissioned a UK artist to create a tender pencil sketch of Freddie for us. Another friend arranged for a felting artist to create a miniature three-dimensional Freddie, so life-like it was both thrilling and heartbreaking to see. Family therapists Ken Dolan-Del Vecchio and Nancy Saxton-Lopez, authors of *The Pet Loss Companion*, a wise book that had helped Rudi and me in our darkest days, sent an inscribed copy to us. They gave us much needed support while also sharing Freddie's story on their podcast to help others grappling with the life-stopping loss we were experiencing.

Camilla, the Duchess of Cornwall, wife of Prince Charles (now King Charles III and Queen Camilla), sent us a note. In 2018, as president of Brooke Action for Working Horses and Donkeys, she had honored my biography of founder Dorothy Brooke by reading from the book at a Brooke Carols Service in Guards' Chapel, London. The copy I gave her showed me with Freddie on the dust jacket, a happy choice of my editor at Allen & Unwin, and I had included Freddie's pawtograph in the book. Her note was handwritten, every word expressing an understanding of the loss of a beloved dog and of how much they give us, unbidden, generously, with all their heart and soul.

Another note arrived from Dame Joanna Lumley, former Bond girl, *Absolutely Fabulous* star, host of a colorful travel series for British television, and animal welfare advocate (she had written a jacket endorsement for my biography of Dorothy Brooke). Her kind, compassionate words came just at a time when Rudi and I were at our lowest point, lighting up the darkness, reminding us of what we had to be grateful for.

Shortly after this book was completed Rudi and I hosted a celebration of life for Freddie, held on September 11, 2022, marking the day of Freddie's adoption in 2010. A few days earlier, Queen Elizabeth II had died, aged 96, at Balmoral Castle in Scotland. We decided to carry on with our gathering, certain that the late queen would be in favour of celebrating the life of a much-loved dog.

Among our guests was my friend Linda Rogers, former poet laureate of Victoria, a much-lauded writer who had helped convince me to write my 2019 biography of Woo, monkey companion of Emily Carr. For Freddie's celebration of life, Linda, who had met Freddie shortly after we adopted him, wrote a poem specially for him. On the page she had sketched a leash that seemed to float above the poem, sparkling with diamantes, like a ring of stars, glued to the collar.

"Freddie was a jewel on earth," she explained, as she prepared to read the poem, alluding to the jeweled collar. "And, as we know, there are no leashes needed in heaven."

Now, Unison
by Linda Rogers

*We aspire to the roof where the view
is inspiring, crows singing in trees,
puppies off leash chasing balls, trees
a mumbling choir, all together now,*

unison, hard to tell them apart.

*We call it wisdom when
we know that loving and
grieving are as close as
sky and the roof of the
world, where beginning
and end are joined by
invisible strings, not leads
with diamond collars shaped*

like crowns but the round
door we pass through
both times, entrance and
exit suffused in radiance,
where everyone, beloved
puppy, crow and Queen
is welcomed to the light.

I collected all the notes, letters, and poems in an old biscuit tin, which I placed under the small oak cabinet that held all Freddie's most intimate things: his collar and tags, his leash and harness, jackets and jumpers he had liked to wear, and things I had saved over the years, like a cardboard tube he had chewed.

We put these things into the chest only a few days after Freddie's passing, then slid its doors shut, only to open them once more a few weeks later when a special toy I'd misplaced needed to go inside. I had to make room for the toy by moving aside the jacket he had last worn. Smelling his familiar smell, I held it to my face. For a few moments, he was with me again. Only the senses can carve out of thin air, on the thinnest possible stimuli, the fully rounded being we'd loved and lost. It was only with the greatest effort that I folded the garment and put it back inside the chest.

Preserving a cardboard tube Freddie had chewed a decade earlier may seem to some pointless and not a little absurd. So, I would venture to say, is the saving and celebrating of saints' relics, of pressed roses cut from a vanished garden, old photos and letters and more durable objects like that endearing sculpture of a dog at the feet of my ancestress Tamburga von Hutten. But these gestures of remembrance, moments of captured past, signposts perhaps leading to nowhere, all proceed from love, which even those more rational folks have to admit continues past the death of the beloved. And, as most of us also know, love, though sometimes misguided, is never wrong.

WHAT STOOD OUT AMONG the outpouring of sympathy was a book sent to us by my friend Maria Goodavage, author of *Top Dog, Soldier Dogs*, and *Doctor Dogs*, among other *New York Times* bestselling books. Like many who loved him, Maria had made a special effort to come meet Freddie (and me) in Vancouver while we still lived in the West End, bringing inscribed copies of her books to Freddie (and us).

Normally shy with people he didn't know, Freddie turned his chocolate pudding eyes on Maria almost from the moment she arrived. Years earlier, I had tried to console Maria after the passing of her beloved dog Jake, telling her what we had done to help ease our anguish when Jessie died. She reminded me of this when, in an email I sent her shortly after Freddie left, I had confessed that life was not worth living without my little friend in it to love and care for.

I had alerted Maria a few years earlier to a book I had intended to use as the basis of another canine biography. The project had fallen through, but I found the book moving and believed Maria would think so, too. The book, *Beautiful Joe's Paradise, or, The Island of Brotherly Love*, was the sequel to *Beautiful Joe,* written by the Canadian novelist Margaret Marshall Saunders (1861–1947).

Beautiful Joe, published in 1893, was the first Canadian novel to sell a million copies. It tells the story of a dog Saunders had actually met, in Meaford, Ontario, in about 1892. The dog had been abused by his guardian, who had cut off his ears and tail. The dog came to live with Saunders's relatives in the town. He was known for a number of amazing feats, including alerting a family to a fire in their home and foiling burglars. He was called Beautiful Joe because, while his former guardian had tortured and disfigured him, Joe did not hold this against the rest of the human race.

In the sequel I had mentioned to Maria, *Beautiful Joe's Paradise*, a boy called Sam Emerson lives in San Francisco in the 1900s with his widowed mother and his bull terrier, Ragtime. One day a neighbor boy kills Ragtime with a stone. Sam won't let his mother bury the dog, and that night, Sam dreams of taking a trip with the deceased Ragtime by hot air balloon, in the company of other animals, including monkeys, up over Mount Tamalpais to an island where all animals go when they die, where there is harmony and peace and love. Ragtime is brought back to life there, and Sam meets all the animals, including their leader, who is none other than Beautiful Joe, his ears and tail restored. Paradise in Saunders's book means that all the animals harmed on earth are like the ones I saw in the dream I had just before Freddie decided he could trust me—though broken in life, they are returned to their normal selves in heaven, abuse and disfigurement eradicated. On awakening, Sam finds he's been in a kind of coma, with the doctor and his mother hovering near his bed, and he resolves to be kinder not just to animals but to humans; he becomes a junior member of the San Francisco SPCA.

For people like Maria and me, the heaven of religious faith was still on the docket, "in need of more proof," but we could get behind a heaven for animals, a place they deserve after all they have done for humankind in their too-short lives. And the book moved me for another reason: on a trip with Freddie to San Francisco, we had walked up to the base of Mount Tamalpais one golden evening, and though Freddie was tired from a day of sightseeing, he kept wanting to proceed up the mountain. Les and I both laughed and asked, "What's up there? Squirrels?"

What was up there for him? I'd give anything to know.

Shortly after Freddie's death, Maria sent Rudi and me one of her last copies of an early picture book she'd written for children, *Dog Heaven: Somewhere Over the Rainbow Bridge*. With colorful illustrations of dogs and their humans, it is about how people often grieve when their dogs die, and how dogs try to tell us that crossing the rainbow bridge is a beautiful thing, with angels to care for them there. In her book, the dogs know, anticipate, the day when their human can join them.

The last line in the book still moves me: "It just wouldn't be heaven without your best friend."[3] It was lovely to think of Freddie in a place of no fear, no pain, where he could breathe without effort and run as he loved to do, where he wasn't worried about us because he knew we would join him soon. I was reminded of a story from years back about British Conservative MP Alan Kenneth Mackenzie Clark (1928–1999), who came close to being converted to Catholicism but held back when informed that his dogs were unwelcome in heaven. Well then, he said, I can do without that paradise.[4] Will Rogers would have agreed. He famously said, "If there are no dogs in heaven, then when I die I want to go where they went."

Even if a heaven of animals, or a heaven of humans with animals, is a fantasy, I am reminded of something I did not always realize while Freddie was with us, but which seems crystal clear to me now: Having Freddie in our lives, helping him learn to trust, showing him he need not fear the world, and learning from him all we ever need to know about courage and trust—all this had already been heaven on earth.

Epilogue

There only remains the recollection of
an unquenchable vitality and capacity for life,
above all of love and loyalty, and of something
for want of a better word I can only
call nobility.

SIR ARTHUR BRYANT[1]

T HROUGHOUT MY LIFETIME OF almost sixty years, I have had strange experiences with significant dates. As a biographer, I'd noticed patterns in the lives of the people I studied. Birthdays, christening dates, or marriages so often coincide with crucial events, times when an individual is pushed to the wall and must overcome obstacles of scenario and self, sometimes facing life-altering injury or death, or the resolution of some old pain.

I had noticed these coincidences—or are they?— in my own life. What alignment of stars gave Freddie his first cancer diagnosis on the same day, twenty-three years later, of my own cancer surgery? What entity, like the roving clownish devil of the Book of Job, lit on

Freddie's final Gotcha Day, in summer 2021, for his first chemotherapy treatment of his second, shortest but most courageous cancer journey? A day that had always been one of joy and thanks and it ended like this?

And what, I had to ask, had put me on the highway heading north to Sidney, the same day a year later, a dog sitting in the backseat of the car? There he was, when I glanced in the rear-view mirror: brown eyes, so like Freddie's, shining out of a face characterized, as Freddie's was, by a long triangle of a spitz nose. He seemed to return my gaze, and for an unthinking instant it was possible to believe he was giving me one of those looks of love that Freddie specialized in, depth after golden depth of something indefinable, welling with sweetness, interest, sympathy.

This was not possible, of course, where this dog was concerned. He was a spitz, like Freddie, though white where Freddie was dark, but there had not been a swiftly beating heart in that dusty chest for 102 years. Why was this? Because the dog in my back seat was Muggins, the once famed and forgotten fundraising hero of World War I–era Victoria, once thought lost, now only recently rediscovered in serendipitous circumstances that had to be seen to be believed.

I still have a hard time thinking of the story of Muggins's rediscovery as real. Sylvia van Kirk, the Muggins scholar who had chosen me to write his life, put it best. "I can't believe this isn't a dream," she told me.

Paul Jenkins, the volunteer coordinator of the Victoria History Project for the Canadian Red Cross BC-Yukon, emailed me in June 2022 to say that a man in Langford believed he might have Muggins's stuffed and mounted body. His family had had the figure for many years; he and his brother remembered it being in their living room when they were boys, and it had then gone into the attic at some point, which is where it was rediscovered.

As exciting and incredible as this sounded, I was disinclined to believe this could remotely be true. Sylvia and I had both heard on good authority that because of the way the mounted body of Muggins had been handled over the years, sitting in hot storefront windows and on the sidewalk outside the Red Cross Superfluities Shop on Douglas Street throughout World War II, it had simply disintegrated. In all Sylvia's years of research and talking to locals, including members of the family of Muggins's guardian, Beatrice Woodward, this was the conclusion everyone drew.

It made sense to me. I had inherited a fur opera cape, made in the 1930s, from my grandmother. (We kept the cape, which I had been planning to either donate to an animal shelter or give a dignified burial, because Freddie had stretched out on it one evening when I'd put it on the floor, and it became his go-to comfort blanket when he was stressed.) After years of improper storage in a dry climate, the sealskin had taken on the strange consistency of cardboard and had only resumed its original softness after I moved to the humid air of the British Columbia coast.

Knowing what temperature variations had done to alter the structure of my grandmother's cape, despite its origins in the studio of one of the best furriers in Southern California, I could not imagine how a mounted figure of a dog, exposed for years to heat, damp, and people touching it, could then have survived whole in a Langford attic, where it had allegedly been stored for over sixty years. Attics in this part of North America can be blazing hot in summer, freezing cold in winter. There are bugs, there's dust, there's mold. All of this made me hesitate to accept this figure as being that of Muggins; it was likely another dog, stuffed and mounted much later. I didn't want—couldn't handle—any more disappointment of hopes.

That said, there was only one way to determine just what we were dealing with. Paul asked Sylvia and me to come to his house in Victoria, where he was keeping the figure, and have a look at it to be sure.

The family told Paul that they had happened to see an interview I had done at the time of my book's release, in autumn 2021, televised by a Victoria news station. I had brought to the interview a 1917 postcard photograph of Muggins (taken when he was still alive) that I acquired from a rare book dealer in the United States. That, along with the other images of the dog used in my book, convinced the family that the dog they had was the same one. It was something of a miracle the figure had been found at all, they explained. One of the brothers was looking in the attic and his flashlight happened to catch the gleam of a pair of brown eyes.

On our arrival at Paul's house, Sylvia and I sat just outside his garage door, shielded from the hot afternoon sun by an umbrella. He served us something cold to drink while we chatted. I tried not to get too excited, and Sylvia was of the same mind. "It's hard to take in," she told me. "Can this be real?"

Then Paul said, holding up a remote device, "Are you ready?" At our nod, he pushed the control button, like Monty Hall opening door number three. Up went the garage door, panel after folding panel, whirring and clanking. And suddenly, there he was, on a stained wooden plinth still stamped with the name of the respected Victoria taxidermist who had preserved him for eternity. *Muggins*.

I had already imagined, being a writer, what this moment might be like, and how I would frame it. "There was Muggins, or what was left of him." But not now. He was all there, or almost. One of his pointed ears was missing; the other was hanging by a thread. His once bright white coat was dusty as a pharaoh's mummy, as dirty as can be imagined for a dog who had not had a bath for a century. His black nose was scuffed.

I had the 1917 postcard with me, and I held it up in front of the figure before us. Not only was there no mistaking the unique features of paws, muzzle, body configuration and size, but the taxidermist had clearly worked from this famous photo, which had been reprinted all over the world in Muggins's heyday: facing forward but body positioned toward the left of the photo, feet gracefully placed, tail a white plume from behind, head erect, and eyes—those "speaking eyes," as one journalist of the war years called them— gazing straight ahead, keenly awaiting what task was expected of him next. All that was needed to com- pletely match the postcard was the harness and two Fry's cocoa tins (now lost) that served as collection boxes, the Red Ensign under his feet and the Union Jack behind, and nothing really had changed since the Great War.

The little dog that had been lauded by a future British monarch, posed with General Sir Arthur Currie, been petted by the cream of Victoria society, had had

medals pinned to his harness, was awarded an honor-
ary first lieutenancy by the American Navy aboard a ship
sailing the waves of the Pacific Ocean—far from being a
victim of neglect, he was still here.

Which brings me back to the dog we had just lost.

Rudi and I had slowly begun to adjust to a life in
which we would never again see Freddie. What remained
of his physical self was now ashes in a blue satin bag in
a ceramic urn topped with a miniature portrait of him.
"How do you want him to look?" the artist asked me.
As he was in his last moments, I told her, when despite
being gravely ill, he stood upon seeing us enter the ICU,
and though he could hardly breathe, continued to stand
for us until going to sleep in our arms. We had just begun
to stop expecting him to be there at home, waiting for
us at the door. I had come to a rather cold conclusion,
which no doubt, looking back now, was as much defense
mechanism as embraced philosophy. More and more,
as I lost loved ones, and grow older myself, I schooled
myself to accept that death really is the end.

I told myself that there is nobody in the great beyond
looking down, lovingly or judgingly, on us, pulling strings
to help us or trip us up; once the body dies, out goes
the candle, never to be lit again. I told myself that on
some level, we who write, paint, compose, dance, act, all
know this, with our cat's sense of the mouse of homely
reality scuffling behind the attractive wallpaper of make-
believe. That when we are moved to get down on paper
or stage or canvas that which stimulates our imagination and prompts us to say what must be said, shown,
played, and make its existence known, it is because we
know that when we leave this place, it's over; the creative act is one sure way to feel that we have in theory,

if not in fact, made some part of ourselves immortal. And that the help we think we're receiving in return for prayers or incense or charitable donations is not from somebody "up there" but rather is us putting into practice in our own lives what we learned from those who loved us. Honoring through remembering. Paying the love forward.

But I couldn't shake off something else—that seductive sense that something had been divinely ordered. Was it all really just a tissue of coincidence, reordered into a falsely coherent pattern by wishful thinking, by the human need to put a story between ourselves and the wholly unpredictable circumstances of life? "What day did the family contact you?" I asked Paul. He told me, and when I made the connection, I had one of those frissons of joy that power our belief in a magical world where there are no coincidences. "That," I replied, "was the day my first royalty cheque for *Muggins* arrived." From that large cheque, I'd given seventy percent to the BCSPCA, in memory of Freddie and Muggins, and the balance to the Canadian Red Cross of BC-Yukon, which still regards Muggins as its mascot.

"He does need to be cleaned up a little," smiled Sylvia, and Paul said, "I wonder if he can be."

I said, like the kid raising his hand first in class, "I'll research a restorer." Furthermore, I said, I'd pay for the work. The money in my savings, inherited from Bill and used to help Freddie fight his cancer battle, would now help to bring Muggins back to life.

So it was that I found myself driving back to Sidney, with a pair of brown eyes looking at mine from the back seat. When I arrived home, I set Muggins down on the same round Chinese rug that Freddie had dozed on for years beside my desk, now in front of our hearth. Rudi and I sat and looked at him.

He was not the first dog we'd had in the house since Freddie's death. That had been a friend's black and white Staffy, Molly. She'd come to tea with her guardians and was instantly drawn to the contents of Freddie's toy box, which we kept in the living room in the same place Freddie had known it. Not only did Molly select Freddie's favorite toys, but she was playing with them almost as if he was playing too. She ran toward an unseen play-mate across the room, brandishing the toy, then ran back to us—once she even dropped the toy and looked up as if to encourage a playmate to take it. I again envied the superior senses of dogs. How often had Rudi and I looked up, one of us saying, "Did you hear him cough just now?" or "What was that?" or felt, in the night, the shift of a small body on the bed, rolling over on its back? Molly seemed to know things we could only guess at.

Unsurprisingly, with Muggins's figure in our living room, the sense that we weren't alone was heightened. The feeling continued as we drove our car onto a ferry to take him across the Salish Sea to the mainland, where I had located a taxidermy restorer.

I had stopped counting the number of times we had made this sailing with Freddie during his months of chemotherapy. Usually, when you board an ocean liner, you feel an excitement throughout the voyage about where you will disembark, the experiences that await you in a place you've never been to. Sailing on a ferry from Vancouver Island to the mainland, however, was normally a workaday journey from point A to point B, toward all that was familiar on the other side. But each trip with Freddie had been like a new journey, powered by hope, at the end of which was an experience that could be good, could be bad, could never be second-guessed, but was at least the act of doing something. And today, as we sat on the upper deck with another dog in the back seat, covered in a cloth lest he draw unwanted attention, it felt a lot the same. Would the end of this journey fix another little dog in need of repair?

We pulled up to the studio of the restorer, Max of Dulchis Mortem Taxidermy, in a hilly suburb of Mission, and I carefully carried Muggins out of the car and into a garage where I placed him on a table for Max to examine. I found myself talking about Muggins the way I used to do when we handed Freddie over to the masked vet techs at the oncologist's in Langley; found myself stroking the figure's matted, dusty coat, touching the battered nose and paws with their white claws—as with Freddie, not wanting to let go.

Then we went back to the car, and as I backed out of the driveway, I saw Max drape plastic over the figure and carry Muggins gently away. I began to cry, as I had never dared to do when watching Freddie being taken into the clinic, never wanting him to see my despair, praying the therapeutic poisons I had authorized to be dripped into his veins would kill what was bad and give more time to what was good. It didn't help that we had delivered Muggins on the same day Freddie had been rescued in Kamloops twelve years earlier—again that strange synchronicity.

On this trip, Rudi and I had arranged to visit SAINTS (Senior Animals in Need Today Society), the farm outside Mission where, ten years before, Les and I had taken Freddie to meet the animals who had been rescued from neglect and abuse. After leaving Muggins with Max, we pulled up to the wooden fencing, parked, and sat in the car for a few minutes. We were early, and I was still shaken from dropping off Muggins.

"You're thinking he's Freddie," Rudi told me. "That we're waiting for the call to come pick him up. This is Muggins. And Max said he won't be ready for a few months. Just relax."

He was right. I was also contending with other memories. Sitting there with the car windows open, we heard the lowing of a cow, reminding me of what had happened that day of my first visit ten years before. Les and I had carried Freddie up to the fence to see Emily, the black-and-white spotted cow who, as a calf, had been rescued from a kill pen a few years earlier. Spotting us, Emily had broken into a run, like a dog eager for pats or treats, and before we knew what was happening, she had pushed her snout through the boards and had licked Freddie from his belly to his face with one swipe. Freddie, who was learning so many new things with us, had looked at us as if to say, "Is this something I need to know about?" But we—cow, dog, humans—were as suffused in happiness as we were in summer sunshine.

Rudi and I walked up the driveway, where we were met by Kate Lennan, the operations manager. A tall blonde woman with a bright, kind smile, Kate guided us around the paddocks to meet everyone there. Emily was gone—she had died only a week or so before our visit—but new residents came to see us: a young and feisty calf (who chewed on my shoe); Ziggy the donkey, who had the gift of soothing new residents in need of a friend; Elvis the goat, strutting in all his glory. I had been looking forward to greeting another SAINT who was no longer there. I'd met Mystic, a rambunctious Samoyed, on that first visit in 2010. She had just arrived at SAINTS that year, a palliative puppy with what was diagnosed as a life-limiting health challenge that gave her, at most, a year. When she made it to her first birthday, SAINTS staff had thrown Mystic a birthday party, pulling out all the stops because, of course, the diagnosis had indicated that she had very little time left. To everyone's surprise, she lived on, racing around the property with her battered stuffies, increasingly the prankster and showing no signs of disappearing any time soon. Mystic was taken to the vet for another examination, and it was discovered that though her kidneys were malformed, they worked just fine. So the little pup who'd been living on borrowed time had grown up and lived it up, spoiled rotten, for the next twelve years, passing away two months before our August visit. "She had a wonderful life," Kate told me, "just what we promise them when they come to us." I could see that that was the case not just for Mystic and Emily but for the horses and pigs and chickens we met along the way. Though each had had sometimes very sad lives before coming to SAINTS, my mood lifted when I saw how well they were doing in a caring and loving environment, putting me firmly back down in the present moment, where animals always are.

Rudi and I had just reached a point where we could talk about Freddie without that tightening of the throat, and we'd decided we were ready for this visit, which would involve meeting elderly dogs, some of whom might remind us of Freddie in his last days. "Here's where the Littles live," said Kate, showing us into the farmhouse and down a hallway to a door that opened into a room bright with sunshine. I remembered the small dogs I had met here a decade ago. Leaving Freddie outside with Les—apart from Freddie's fear of other dogs, we didn't want to expose him to any viruses or illness among the residents—I'd sat on the linoleum floor off the kitchen, welcoming the tousled Maltese dogs and poodles and pugs that, discarded in their elder years, now creaky, slow, some with coughs, scuttled across to meet me. Some were deaf, some unable to see, but they knew somebody was there for them. They were trusting, despite being given no reason whatsoever to do so, based on what they had experienced of humans before SAINTS. They had a courage that I was not sure I myself would be able to summon after similar neglect, abuse, or abandonment.

Rudi and I came into the same room, sat on the same floor, saw poodles, Maltese, and pugs, their cloudy eyes swiveling toward us, noses lifted to catch our scent. Slowly, one and then another got up from their beds to greet us. It is true that Rudi and I were now able to actually talk about Freddie, and in part this was because we had begun to discuss adopting another dog. There was in fact not so much an *if*—we both wanted and intended to help another dog in need by giving it a loving home— but very much a *when* involved with that conversation. When would we know we were ready to open our home and hearts to another dog needing both? When would we be able to plan for another adoption without pangs of guilt and irrational fears that we were somehow replacing Freddie, erasing him? When would we know that in saving another life, we were not forgetting his?

A little dog, a sort of dustmop on four uncertain legs, tottered toward me, bright eyes gleaming through dark grey fur silvered with age, and a quixotic thought came to mind of a piece of embroidery we had hanging on a wall at home, as old in decades as this dog was in human years. Stitched after the outbreak of the Second World War by a child in England, the framed panel had caught my eye in a corner of an antiques shop on Vancouver Island. It bore across its unadorned canvas face lines from the famous Christmas message broadcast by King George VI in 1939, quoting from "God Knows," a poem by Minnie Louise Haskins, published in 1908:

> And I said to the man who stood
> at the gate of the year:
> "Give me a light that I may tread
> safely into the unknown."
> And he replied:
> "Go out into the darkness and put
> your hand into the Hand of God.
> That shall be to you better than light
> and safer than a known way."

Like Freddie, that evening years ago when he came upstairs and down the dark hall to lay his head on my knee and show me that, despite our brief interlude of distance, he did trust me after all, this little dog, unsteady on her feet, uncertain of eyesight, doggedly found her way to me, pushing her snout into my welcoming hands. Mine was no hand of God, but she knew where to find it and that it meant no harm.

"That's Ruby," said Kate. "She was found as a stray."

I lifted Ruby's face to mine and saw trust, and love, both undiminished by her experiences of humankind. "Better than light," I whispered to her, "and safer than a known way."

It was as if Freddie, through Ruby, had given me permission to drop my anguish over his death, as I had once had a chance to drop my anguish over the way he had been abused. He felt as close to me now as Ruby. In that closeness was nothing but joy. And in that joy was a renewed intention of welcoming another rescue pup into our household, whenever or however that might be—perhaps the most important revelation of the experience.[2]

I still hesitate to accept that there is a heaven, even the one that Emily Dickinson spoke of with such certainty that she hoped her dog, Carlo, would be the first to meet her there. But in the words of Sir Arthur Bryant, writing of the stray terrier, Jimmy, who became his beloved canine friend, I found resonance.

> True to his nature as a dog . . . he displayed towards the humans who had befriended him a trust, a selfless tenderness and devotion that nothing could alter and which as much as any experience of life, has convinced me that, in some mysterious way beyond our understanding, love is eternal.[3]

Acknowledgements

Agnes Aaberg, Brian Aaberg, Dr. Christian Bolliger, Dr. Elise Bommer, Dr. Manuel Bommer, Dr. Erinne Branter, Lady Colin Campbell, Dr. Helene Childs, Penny Cooper, Sally Jewell Coxe, Gary Edwards, Melanie Ehrlich, Dr. Kirsten Elliot, Amy Cox Ferriera, Anna Fercoq, Shoni Field, Rev. Daniel Fournier, Nicole Glasrud, Maria Goodavage, Pat Hannah, Les Hayter, Dr. Chamisa Herrera, Carol Hine, Paul Jenkins, Liz Klauser, Rudi Klauser, Dr. Orna Kristal, Crystal Labrie, Daina Liepa, Misty MacGregor, Elizabeth May, Monica Mayse, Dr. Brad McKell, Diane McNally, Ronda Menzies, Sean William Menzies, Dr. Kelli Mulley, Kathleen Paar, Megan Pace, Vivienne Peterson, Melissa Prystupa, Charmaine Quinn, Ian Redmond, Linda Rogers, Ann Searight, Chris Stephen, Jill Stuckey, Posie Sutton-Lieder, Janet Thompson, Dr. Zazie Todd, Dr. Sylvia van Kirk, Rick Van Krugel.

Especial thanks to Niko, our new rescue pup, who sat beside my desk (and often requested that I hold him as I worked, meaning much of the editing was done with one typing hand—excuse typos!), as Freddie once did for earlier volumes, through the final edits of this book.

Heartfelt thanks to the staffs of West End Animal Clinic, City Pets, WAVES, Boundary Bay Veterinary Specialty Hospital, Sidney Animal Hospital, and VCA Canada Central Victoria Veterinary Hospital for looking after Freddie over the years. Your expertise and compassion gave Freddie more time, made a difficult situation bearable for him, and comforted us on the darkest days. We are grateful to all of you.

Notes

PROLOGUE

1. Maureen Adams, *Shaggy Muses: The Dogs Who Inspired Virginia Woolf, Emily Dickinson, Elizabeth Barrett Browning, Edith Wharton, and Emily Brontë* (New York: Ballantine Books, 2007), 14.

2. Helen Humphreys, *And a Dog Called Fig: Solitude, Connection, the Writing Life* (New York: Farrar, Straus and Giroux, 2022), 215.

CHAPTER 1

1. Nina Strawser, "Joe's Escape," unpublished manuscript (ca. 1969).

CHAPTER 2

1. Alexandra Horowitz, *Inside of a Dog: What Dogs See, Smell, and Know* (New York: Simon & Schuster, 2009), 31.

CHAPTER 3

1. Nicholas Dodman, *The Dog Who Loved Too Much: Tales, Treatments, and the Psychology of Dogs* (New York: Bantam Books, 1996), 106–107.

2. Rowland Johns, ed., *Our Friend the Pomeranian* (New York: E. P. Dutton & Company, 1936), 7.

3. Clever Canine, clevercanine.ca/.

4. Edna Porter, ed., *Double Blossoms: Helen Keller Anthology* (New York: Lewis Copeland, 1931), 26.

5. Porter, *Double Blossoms*, 26.

CHAPTER 4

1. Email correspondence with Denise Meade, 2011–22; email from Shoni Field, August 24, 2022.

2. Labrie to author, September 24, 2022.

3. Dodman, *The Dog*, 107.

4. St. John Lucas, "My Dog," *Current Literature* 44, no. 6 (June 1908): 682.

CHAPTER 7

1. "William Luce, Playwright, Dies at 88; Wrote 'Belle of Amherst,'" *New York Times*, December 13, 2019, https://www.nytimes.com/2019/12/12/theater/william-luce-dead.html.

CHAPTER 8

1. Elizabeth Barrett Browning, *Poems*, The World's Classics 176 (London: Oxford University Press, 1912), 233.

CHAPTER 9

1. J. D. McClatchy, ed., *On Wings of Song: Poems About Birds*, Everyman's Library Pocket Poetry (New York: Knopf, 2000), 30.

2. Teresa J. Rhyne website, https://teresarhyne.com/.

3. Mary Webb, *Fifty-One Poems: Hitherto Unpublished in Book Form* (London: Jonathan Cape, 1946), 23.

4. Hayter-Menzies, "My Brave Companion," *Literary Review of Canada*. 29, no. 10 (December 2021): 40.

5. Garfield, *Dog's Best Friend: The Story of an Unbreakable Bond* (New York: William Morrow, 2020), 253.

6. Maria Goodavage (as Maria Hanson), *Dog Heaven: Somewhere Over the Rainbow Bridge*, illustrated by Dee D'Amico (Bloomington, IN: Balboa Press, 2012), 30.

7. Lady Colin Campbell, *With Love from Pet Heaven, by Tum Tum the Springer Spaniel* (London: Dynasty Press, 2011), 1–2.

EPILOGUE

1. Arthur Bryant, *Jimmy: The Dog in My Life* (London: Lutterworth Press, 1960), 48.

2. In October 2022, two months after our visit, Ruby found a forever home. Meeting Ruby caused a shift in our hearts, and on October 25, 2022, a year after we said goodbye to Freddie, Rudi and I adopted Niko, a poodle cross rescued from a puppy mill. Traumatized and unsocialized at first, he learned to play with

Freddie's toys, and our experience helping Freddie allowed us to teach Niko how to be a happy, healthy dog.

3. Bryant, *Jimmy*, 48.

Bibliography

UNPUBLISHED SOURCES

Diaries of Grant Hayter-Menzies, 2010–21
Medical records of Freddie Klauser-Menzies

PUBLISHED SOURCES

Adams, Maureen. *Shaggy Muses: The Dogs Who Inspired Virginia Woolf, Emily Dickinson, Elizabeth Barrett Browning, Edith Wharton, and Emily Brontë*. New York: Ballantine Books, 2007.

Barrett Browning, Elizabeth. *Poems*. The World's Classics 176. Henry Frowde. London: Oxford University Press, 1912.

Bekoff, Marc. *The Emotional Lives of Animals: A Leading Scientist Explores Animal Joy, Sorrow, and Empathy—and Why They Matter*. Novato, CA: New World Library, 2007.

Bryant, Arthur. *Jimmy: The Dog in My Life*. London: Lutterworth Press, 1960.

Campbell, Lady Colin. *With Love from Pet Heaven*, by Tum Tum the Springer Spaniel. London: Dynasty Press, 2011.

Coren, Stanley. *Do Dogs Dream? Nearly Everything Your Dog Wants You to Know.* New York: W.W. Norton & Company, Inc., 2012.

——. *The Intelligence of Dogs: Canine Consciousness and Capabilities.* New York: The Free Press, 1994.

Dodman, Nicholas. *The Dog Who Loved Too Much: Tales, Treatments, and the Psychology of Dogs.* New York: Bantam Books, 1996.

Dolan-Del Vecchio, Ken, and Nancy Saxton-Lopez. *The Pet Loss Companion: Healing Advice from Family Therapists Who Lead Pet Loss Groups.* North Charleston, SC: CreateSpace, 2013.

Forster, Margaret. *Elizabeth Barrett Browning.* London: Chatto & Windus, 1988.

Garfield, Simon. *Dog's Best Friend: The Story of an Unbreakable Bond.* New York: William Morrow, 2020.

Goodavage, Maria (as Maria Hanson). *Dog Heaven: Somewhere Over the Rainbow Bridge.* Illustrated by Dee D'Amico. Bloomington, IN: Balboa Press, 2012.

Hawn, Roxanne. *Heart Dog: Surviving the Loss of Your Canine Soul Mate.* Published by Roxanne Hawn, 2015.

Hayter-Menzies, Grant. *From Stray Dog to World War I Hero: The Paris Terrier Who Joined the First Division.* Lincoln, NB: Potomac Books, 2015.

——. *The Lost War Horses of Cairo: The Passion of Dorothy Brooke.* London: Allen & Unwin, 2018.

——. *Muggins: The Life and Afterlife of a Canadian Canine War Hero.* Victoria, BC: Heritage House, 2021.

——. "My Brave Companion." *Literary Review of Canada.* 29, no. 10 (December 2021): 40.

——. *Woo, the Monkey Who Inspired Emily Carr: A Biography.* Madeira Park, BC: Douglas & McIntyre, 2019.

Horowitz, Alexandra. *Inside of a Dog: What Dogs See, Smell, and Know.* New York: Simon & Schuster, 2009.

Humphreys, Helen. *And a Dog Called Fig: Solitude, Connection, the Writing Life.* New York: Farrar, Straus and Giroux, 2022.

Johns, Rowland, ed. *Our Friend the Pomeranian.* New York: E. P. Dutton & Company, 1936.

Kavin, Kim. *Little Boy Blue: A Puppy's Rescue from Death Row and His Owner's Journey for Truth.* Happauge, NY: Barron's Educational Series, Inc., 2012.

Klam, Julie. *You Had Me at Woof: How Dogs Taught Me the Secret of Happiness.* New York: Riverhead Books, 2010.

Kohl, Jana. *A Rare Breed of Love: The True Story of Baby and the Mission She Inspired to Help Dogs Everywhere.* New York: Simon & Schuster, 2008.

Lucas, St. John. "My Dog." *Current Literature* 44, no. 6 (June 1908): 682.

McClatchy, J. D., ed. *On Wings of Song: Poems About Birds.* Everyman's Library Pocket Poetry. New York: Knopf, 2000.

Porter, Edna, ed., *Double Blossoms: Helen Keller Anthology.* New York: Lewis Copeland, 1931.

Rogers, Linda. "Now, Unison: For Freddie and His Papas." Unpublished, September 11, 2022.

Sandomir, Richard. "William Luce, Playwright, Dies at 88; Wrote 'The Belle of Amherst,'" *New York Times,* December 13, 2019, https://www.nytimes.com/2019/12/12/theater/william-luce-dead.html.

Saunders, Marshall. *Beautiful Joe's Paradise: Or, The Island of Brotherly Love, A Sequel to Beautiful Joe.* London: Jarrold & Sons, 1902.

Schalk, Carl (lyrics) and Vajda, Jaroslav J. (music). *God of the Sparrow, God of the Whale.* 1983.

Strawser, Nina J. "Joe's Escape." Unpublished manuscript, ca. 1969.

Thomas, Abigail. *A Three Dog Life: A Memoir.* New York: Harcourt, Inc., 2006.

Thomas, Elizabeth Marshall. *The Hidden Life of Dogs.* New York: Houghton Mifflin Co., 1993.

Von Kreisler, Kristen. *The Compassion of Animals: True Stories of Animal Courage and Kindness.* Rocklin, CA: Prima Publishing, 1997.

Webb, Mary. *Fifty-One Poems: Hitherto Unpublished in Book Form.* London: Jonathan Cape, 1946.